Power BI
Business Intelligence Clinic
Create and Learn

Roger F. Silva

Roger F. Silva

contact.createandlearn@gmail.com

createandlearn.net

www.linkedin.com/in/roger-f-silva

Power BI version: 64-bit (October 2020)

ISBN: 9781726793216

Contents

For more **Create and Learn** books, visit
www.createandlearn.net:

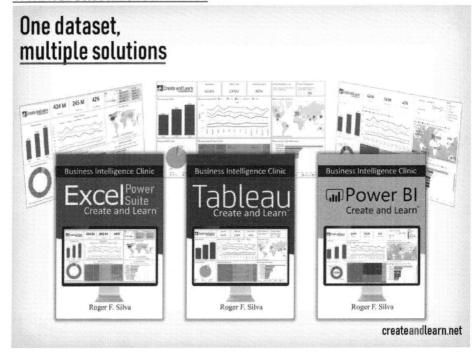

Dashboard to be created: Desktop version

Dashboard to be created: Mobile version

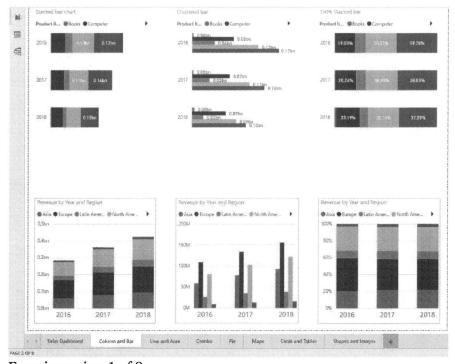

Exercise series: 1 of 8

1. Introduction

Dear Reader,

In this Business Intelligence Clinic series, you will explore various BI solutions.

Each book is about a different BI tool, and you will follow step-by-step instructions to create a professional sales dashboard with the same friendly dataset. This BI Clinic series will help you to compare different Business Intelligence tools, learn the basics, and select the best for your project, company, customers, or personal needs.

In this Create and Learn book: Power BI – Business Intelligence Clinic, you will go through important topics of Microsoft Power BI Desktop, a Free BI tool from Microsoft. You will learn how to install Power BI Desktop, get data from Excel, model your data, work with visuals and reports, create a sales dashboard, and share your work with others.

We will not go into deep theories as to the purpose of this book, and all Create and Learn material is to make the most of your time and learn by doing.

You will follow step-by-step instructions to create a professional sales dashboard, and eight warm-up dashboards to help you rapidly increase your knowledge.

I hope this book will help you to start your journey in the Business Intelligence world and give you the right tools to begin building professionals reports and dashboards using Microsoft Power BI.

You can find more here https://www.createandlearn.net/pbi

Thank you for creating and learning.

Roger F. Silva

contact.createandlearn@gmail.com

createandlearn.net

www.linkedin.com/in/roger-f-silva

2. Get Started

2.1. Business Intelligence and Power BI

The main goal of Business Intelligence is to help people and companies make better decisions, and according to Wikipedia, business intelligence is a set of methodologies, processes, architectures, and technologies that transform raw data into meaningful and useful information used to enable more effective strategic, tactical, and operational insights and decision-making.

Power BI is a Business Intelligence software that allows users to get data from multiple sources, transform the data, and create reports, dashboards, and many types of visualizations.

Then, the user can share those reports with colleagues and customers across multiple platforms, such as Power BI service, SharePoint, websites, and more.

Until recently, Business Intelligence solutions were aimed at Enterprise-level BI, with complex and costly products, and most of it was done by IT professionals.

Nowadays, you can find a range of self-service BI solutions, and Power BI is one of them. These solutions allow salespeople, analysts, managers, and a variety of professionals to get data, model the data, create visualizations and share them.

2.2. Power BI products

According to Microsoft, Power BI is a suite of business analytics tools that deliver insights throughout your organization. It allows you to connect to hundreds of data sources, simplify data preparation, and drive ad hoc analysis. You can produce beautiful reports, then publish them for your organization to consume on the web and across mobile devices.

Power BI Desktop: This is the main tool used in this book. It is a free solution installed on the computer that allows users to connect the data, prepare and model the data, create reports, and run advanced analytics.

* The Power BI Desktop version used in this book is the 64-bit from October 2020.

Power BI Pro: It allows the user to access all the Power BI service content. The user will access an online portal, where it is possible to create dashboards, share with other Pro users, and publish on the web.

Power BI Premium: It provides dedicated resources to run Power BI for organizations or teams. It gives greater data volume, improved performance, and more widespread distribution.

Power BI Mobile: It offers apps for mobile devices. With mobile apps, users can connect and interact with both on-premises and cloud data.

Power BI Embedded: It integrates Power BI visuals into custom applications. Essentially, it enables companies to use all Power BI visuals and functions, inside their applications as if they were native.

Power BI Report Server: It is the on-premises solution and users can move to the cloud when they need it.

2.3. The Business Intelligence Clinic Dataset

The Business Intelligence Clinic dataset is a friendly, easy-to-read set of four tables containing the high-level sales information from a fictitious company, and they will be used in every BI Clinic book.

These are the tables you will find:

Sales: Contains the main sales data in a three-year range.

Region: Contains countries and regions where the company operates.

SalesManager: Contains the sales manager's names by country.

Dates: Contains the dates and groups of dates.

2.4. Install Power BI Desktop

To install Power BI Desktop on your computer, go to the Microsoft Power BI website. Currently, the address is **powerbi.com**, or you can search for "Power BI" inside the Microsoft main page, which is microsoft.com.

On the Power BI website, you will see multiple links to get the free version, such as **Start Free**, **Sign up free**, and others.

1. Go to Products and select **Power BI Desktop** as the image below.

2. Then, click on **Download Free**.

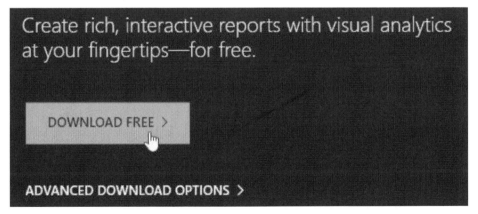

3. If the site redirects you to the Microsoft store. Click **Install** to start the download and the install process.

Open Microsoft Store?

☐ Always open these types of links in the associated app

4. If you have installed Power BI go to **Launch Power BI Desktop** chapter. If not, go to the next step.

5. If you want to download in any different language than English, click on **Advanced Download Options (Download or language options),** and select the language. If not, go to the next step.

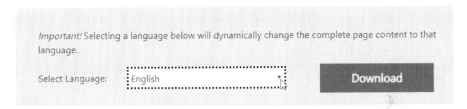

6. If the **Choose the download you want** message appears, select the windows version (usually is x64) and click on **Next.**

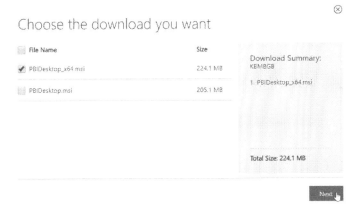

7. After starting the install process, the setup screen will appear. Click on **next**.

8. Read the license agreement, and if you agree, check the box ", I accept the terms and license agreement" and click on **Next**. Also, you have the option to print.

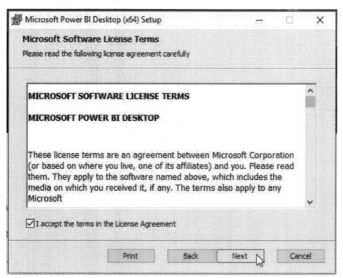

9. Click **Install**.

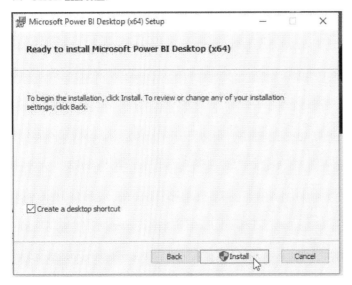

10. Check if you need to click **Yes** to allow Power BI to install and wait till the installation finishes.

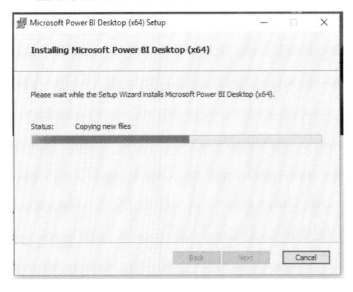

11. Once the installation is completed, leave the box "Launch Microsoft Power BI Desktop" checked and click **Finish**.

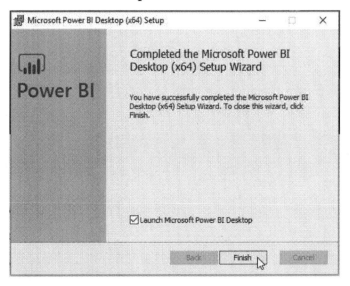

2.5. Launch Power BI Desktop

1. Once you launch Power BI, it will ask you to create a free account.

If you don't want to create an account now, click on **Already have a Power BI account** (bottom) and close the login window.

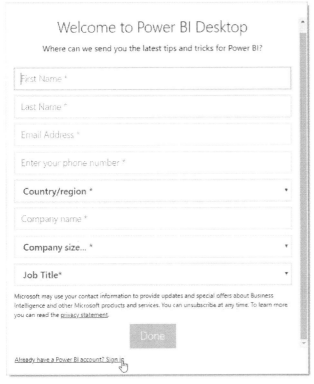

2. Below you will find the start screen, and from here, you can start a new report using the **Get data**, access your recent/pinned reports, **sign in** to your powerbi.com account or **try it free**. We will click on the right top and close this window.

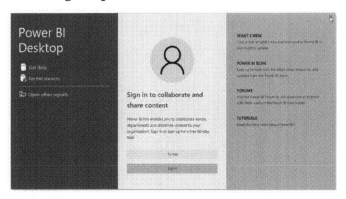

3. The image below shows the first view of Power BI, I will quickly introduce it to you, and as you build your reports, you will get used to most of its tools.

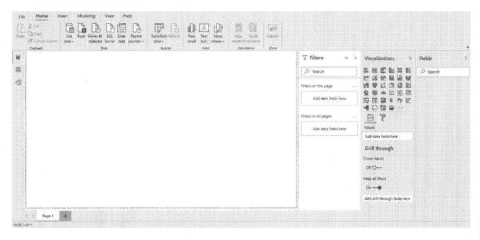

4. The **File** tab is the same that you find in most Microsoft products, where you can create, save, and export your file.

5. The **ribbon** displays common tasks related to visualizations and reports.

6. The Page tab along the bottom, which allows you to select, edit or add a page.

7. The **Report** view, or canvas, where visualizations are created/arranged, followed by **Data** view, where you will find your data, and **Model** (Relationships) view, where you can manage data relationships.

8. The **Visualizations** pane, where you can select visualizations, change colors or axes, drag fields, filters, and more. The **Fields** pane is the place that queries elements, and filters can be dragged to the Report view, and Filters area. The **Filter** pane allows you to create faster filters to be used in a single page or multiple pages across the file.

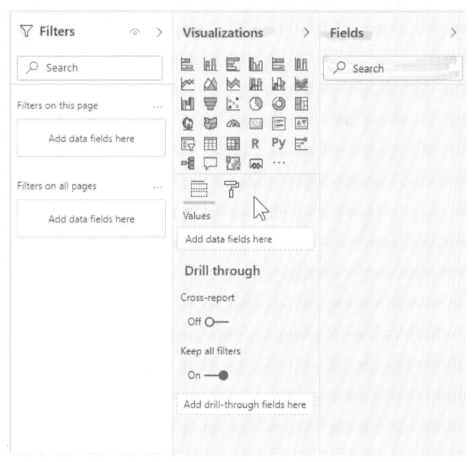

9. Click on the arrow to hide the **Filters** pane.

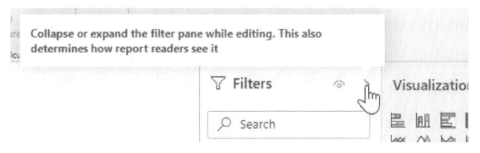

3. Get Data

With Power BI you can connect to different data sources and types. You can use basic sources of data such as CSV files and spreadsheets or online services such as Azure, Salesforce, Dynamics, and much more.

1. Go to **File** tab and save the file as **CL PBI – Sales Dashboard**.

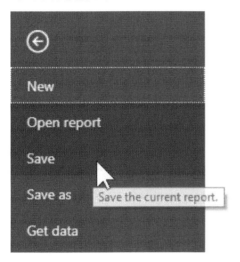

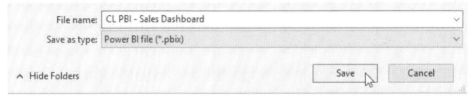

2. Visit the address createandlearn.net/bifiles and download the **SalesData.xlsx**. This file contains the data that you will use for the exercises and dashboard.
   If it asks for a password, type: **bifiles**

Book material:

Right-click the image and click on **Save image as**

SalesData.xlsx

3. Go to **Home** tab and click on **Get Data**.

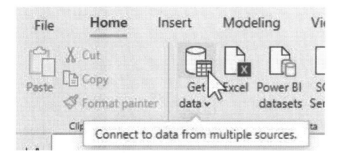

4. Power BI will display all the options to get data. Select **Excel** and click **Connect**.

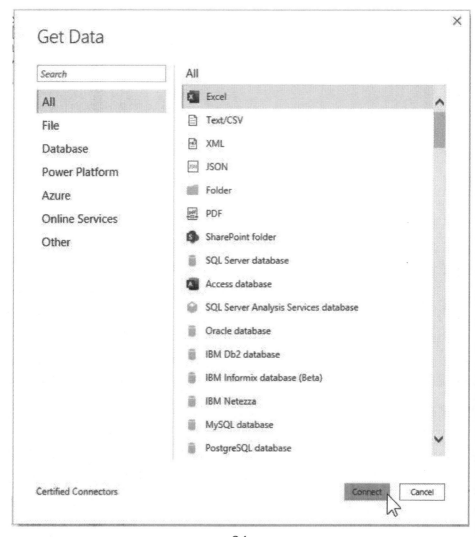

5. Select the **SalesData.xlsx** that you have saved and click **Open**.

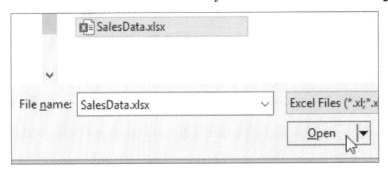

6. The Navigator window will show all available tables. Select all of them by checking their boxes and click on **Load**.

7. In the **Report** view, you will note that the **Fields** list contains every table and columns imported.

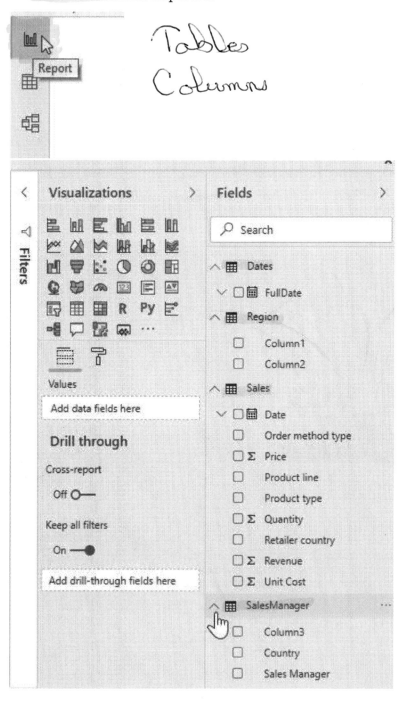

4. Model data

With Power BI you can combine data from multiple sources and set their relationship. Also, you can create custom columns, and calculations making your life much easier and your reports more powerful.

4.1. Fixing Headers

1. Go to **Data** view.

2. Click on **Region** to select this table.

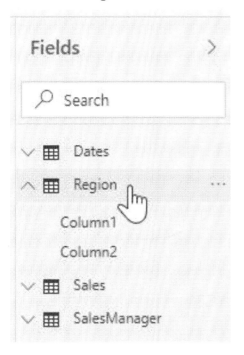

3. You will note that Power BI did not recognize the column names. It usually happens with text columns.

4. To fix the headers, go to **Home** tab, and click on **Transform data** (Edit Queries).

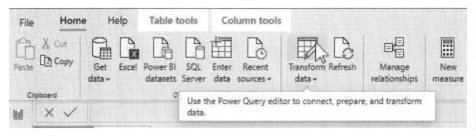

5. Select **Region** table (Queries) and Click on **Use First Row as Headers**. The columns should change to **Country** and **Region**.

6. Click on **Close & Apply**, to leave the query editor and apply the new changes.

4.2. Creating relationships

1. Go to **Model** (Relationships) view.

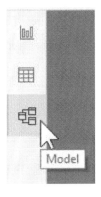

2. To define how **Sales, Region, SalesManager**, and **Dates** will be related. Click on Manage Relationships.

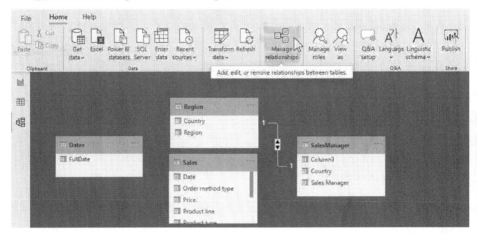

3. Power BI has already related a relationship, but this is not useful for this dashboard. In the **Manage relationships** window select any relationship created and click on **Delete**.

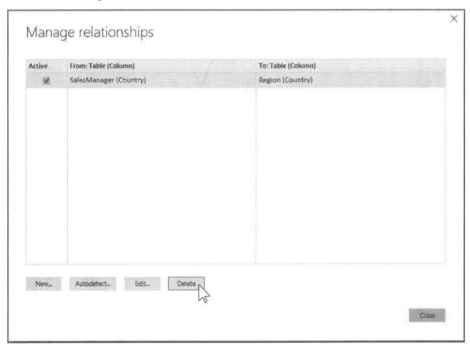

4. Click on **New.**

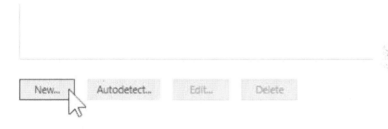

5. Select **Sales** as the top table to be related, and **Region** as the second one.
To relate columns, **click on them,** and they will be highlighted. The example below shows that **Retailer country** will be related to **Country** (BE SURE TO SELECT BOTH COLUMNS). It will help you to tell the region for each sale.

6. For cardinality, select **Many to one (*:1)**, it means that **Many** sales can have only **One** Country/Region for each record/row. See the image below. Click **OK**.

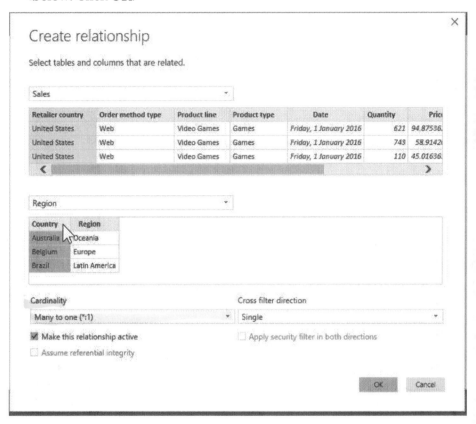

7. Create a new relationship for **Sales** and **SalesManager**, and select **Relailer country**, and **Country** in a **Many to one** relationship like the image below. Then, click **OK**.

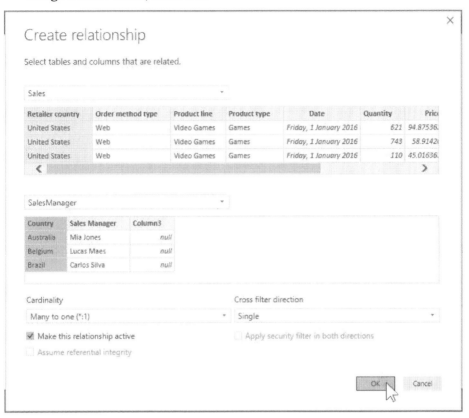

8. Create one more relationship for **Sales** and **Dates,** and select **Date,** and **FullDate** in a **Many to one** relationship like the image below. Then, click **OK.**

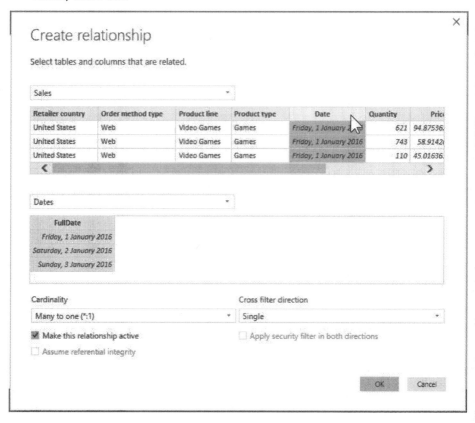

9. The relationships should look like the image below. Click on **Close**.

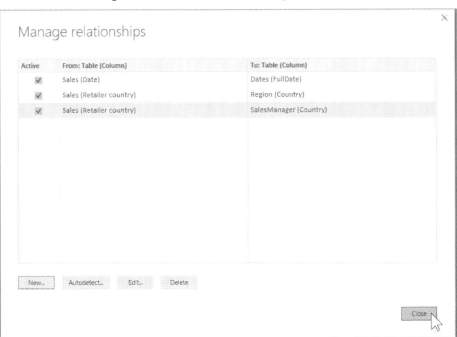

10. The relationship diagram should look like the image below. You can also move the boxes by dragging them. Click on the box title to drag each box.

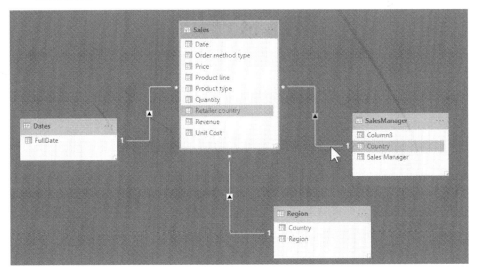

4.3. Formatting Data

1. Go to **Data** view.

2. Select **Sales** table.

3. Click on **Price** column.

Date		Quantity		Price		Revenue		Unit Cost	
Friday, 1 January 2016		621		94.875365...406		58917.6		49.1928753623188	
Friday, 1 January 2016		743		58.914266487214		43773.3		32.5501322341857	
Friday, 1 January 2016		110		45.0163636363636		4951.8		25.25418	
Saturday, 2 January 2016		26		131.642307692308		3422.7		79.4461326923077	

4. Go to **Column tools** (Modeling) tab and click on **Thousands separator**. The price column should have a new format now.

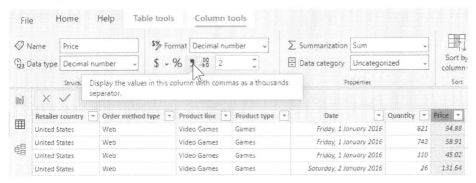

5. Select **Unit Cost** and click on **Thousands separator**. Do the same for **Revenue**.

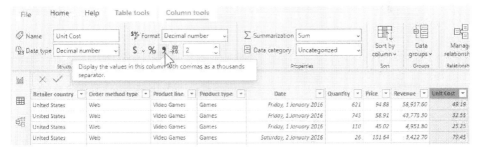

6. Select column **Date**.

oduct type ▼	Date ▼	Quantity ▼	Price ▼
mes	Friday, 1 January 16	621	94.88
mes	Friday, 1 January Date	743	58.91
mes	Friday, 1 January 2016	110	45.02
mes	Saturday, 2 January 2016	26	131.64
mes	Monday, 4 January 2016	115	132.32

7. Click on **Format** and select the format **d/MM/yyyy**.

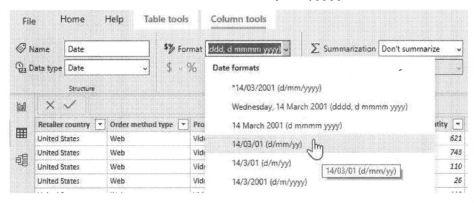

8. The Sales table should be looking like below.

4.4. Creating Calculated Columns

With calculated columns, you can add new data to a table already in your model. But instead of querying and loading values into your new column from a data source, you can create a Data Analysis Expressions (DAX) formula that defines the column's values.

DAX formulas are like Excel formulas. In fact, DAX has many of the same functions as Excel. DAX functions, however, are meant to work over data interactively sliced or filtered in a report, like in Power BI Desktop. Unlike Excel, where you can have a different formula for each row in a table when you create a DAX formula for a new column, it will calculate a result for every row. Column values are recalculated as necessary, such as when the underlying data is refreshed, and values have changed.

1. Select the Sales table, and go to **Home** tab and click on **New Column**.

2. The formula bar will be active. It means that you can now add a formula for your new calculated column.

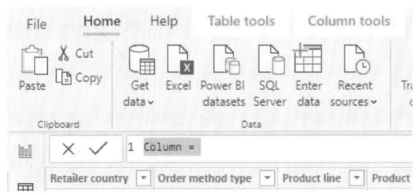

3. Delete any data in the formula bar, and type the formula:

Total Cost = Sales[Unit Cost]*Sales[Quantity]

Then press **Enter**.

See the explanation:

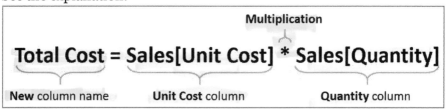

4. Note that as you type, Power BI shows the options compatible. You can click on the correct one when it appears.

5. The column should be as the image below.

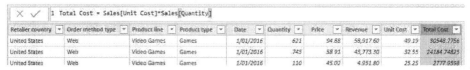

6. To create the **Gross Result** column, click on **New Column**, clean any previous information, and type the formula:

Gross Result = Sales[Revenue] - Sales[Total Cost]

Then, press **Enter**.

7. The two new columns will appear in the **Fields** list under **Sales** table.

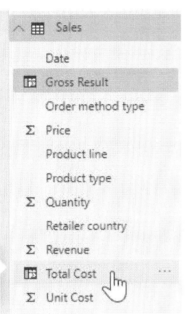

8. Go to **Fields** list and select **Dates**.

9. To create the Month Number column. Click on New Column, and type the formula:
   Month Number = Dates[FullDate].[MonthNo]
   Then, press Enter.

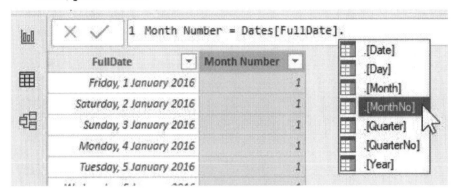

10. To create the **Year** column. Click on **New Column**, and type the formula:

Year = Dates[FullDate].[Year]

Then, press **Enter**.

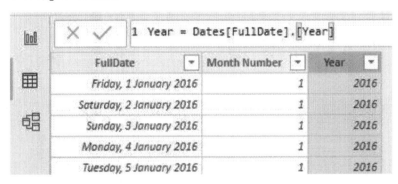

11. To create the **Financial Year** column, you will use the **IF** statement. Click on **New Column**, and type the formula:

FY = if(MONTH(Dates[FullDate])>6,   YEAR(Dates[FullDate])+1, YEAR(Dates[FullDate]))

See the explanation:

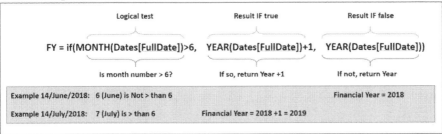

12. The three new columns will appear in the **Fields** list under **Dates** table.

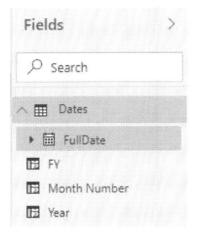

4.5. Creating Measures

Measures are used in some of the most common data analyses for example, sums, averages, minimum or maximum values, counts, or more advanced calculations, you create yourself using a DAX (Data Analysis eXpression) formula. The calculated results of measures are always changing in response to your interactions with your reports, allowing for fast and dynamic ad-hoc data exploration. Let's take a closer look.

1. Go to **Fields** and select **Sales**.

To create the **Gross Result** measure, click on **New Measure** and type the formula:

Gross Result m = sum(Sales[Revenue])-sum(Sales[Total Cost])

Press Enter.

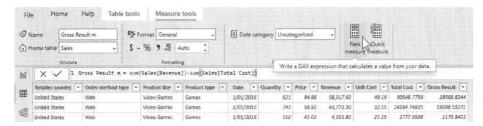

To create the **Gross Margin** measure, click on **New Measure** and type the formula:

Gross Margin = (sum(Sales[Revenue])- sum(Sales[Total Cost])) / sum(Sales[Revenue])

Press Enter.

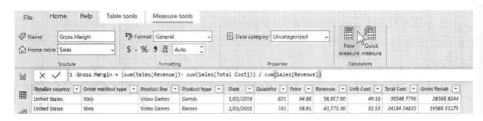

2. Click on **Save**.

*If you want to learn more about DAX visit the articles on https://www.createandlearn.net/biclinicposts

5. Visualizations and Reports

1. Go to **Report**.

2. Right-click the **Page 1** tab and click on **Rename Page**. Type **Sales Dashboard**

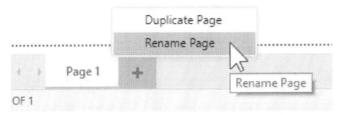

3. Create seven new pages and rename them as [**Column and Bar**], [**Line and Area**], [**Combo**], [**Pie**], [**Maps**], [**Cards and Tables**] and [**Shapes and Images**].

5.2. Column and Bar Charts

1. Select the **Column and Bar** tab.

2. Go to Visualizations and click on **Stacked bar chart.**

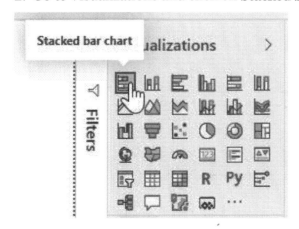

3. Power BI will create a blank visual as the image below.

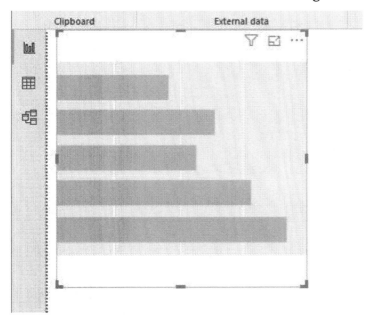

4. Add some data to this new visual by dragging the fields in the **Fields** list and dropping in the specific component. In this chart, the components available are **Axis**, **Legend**, **Value**, and Tooltips. The image below shows the Fields and where they were dragged.
In the **Axis**, component, drag the **Year** field.
In the **Legend** component, drag the **Product line**.
In the **Value** component, drag the **Revenue**.

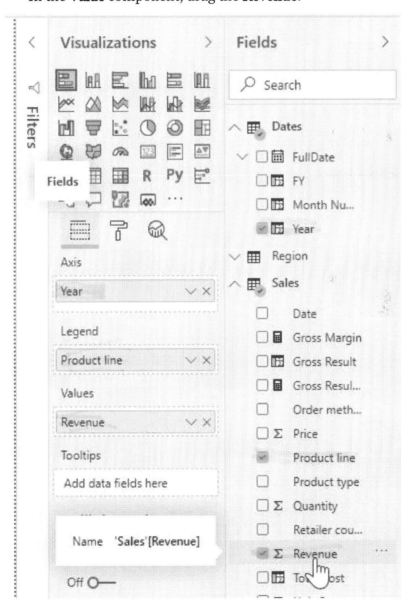

5. The new chart should look like the image below.

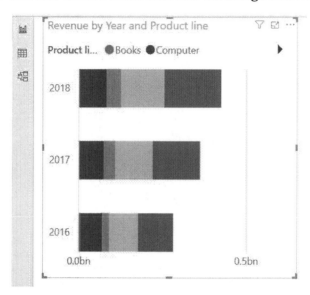

* Colors may vary, but if you want to use the same theme used here go to **View** tab and select the theme **Classic**.

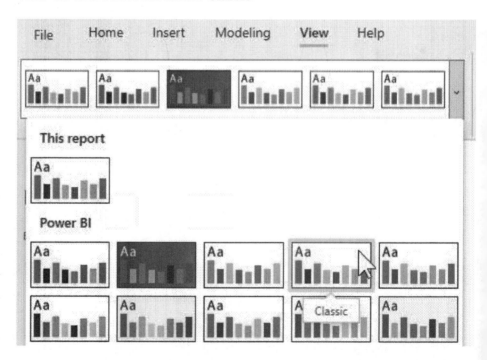

6. Select the chart. Go to **Visualizations** pane and click on **Format** tab.

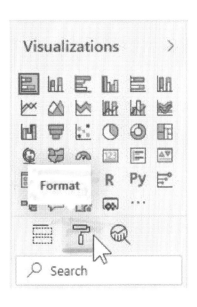

7. Click on **Title** and type in the **Title Text** "Stacked bar chart".

8. Go to **Data labels** and set as **On.**

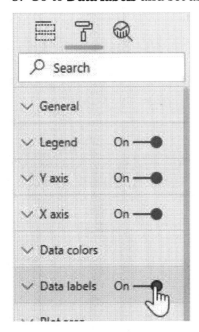

9. Go to **X-Axis** and change to **Off.**

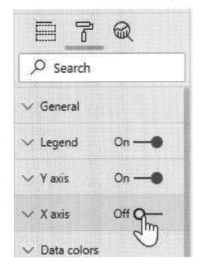

10. Select the chart and go to **Home** tab and click on **Copy.**

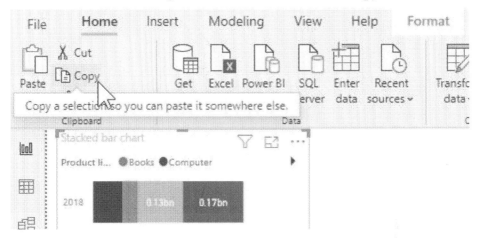

11. Click two times on **Paste**, to have three similar charts as the image below. You can move the charts by dragging and dropping.

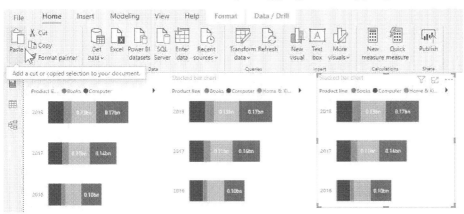

12. To change the type, select the chart in the middle and click on **Clustered bar chart**.

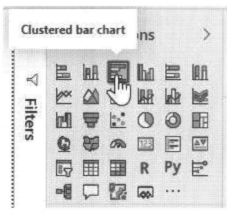

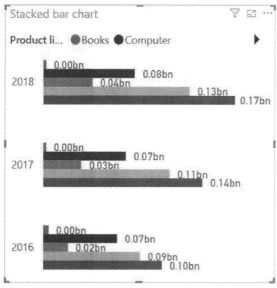

13. Go to **Format** and change the title to **Clustered bar**.

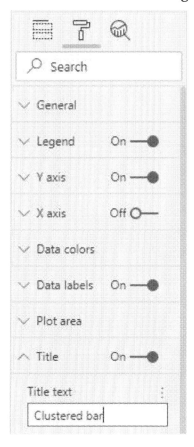

14. Select the third chart and click on **100% Stacked bar chart**. And, change the title to **100% Stacked bar**.

15. The three charts should look like the image below. Note how the same data tell a different story on each chart.

16. Press escape, or click on a blank area on the canvas, to deselect the chart, and click on **Stacked column chart**.

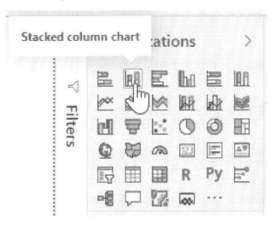

17. Drag the fields **Year**, **Region,** and **Revenue** to the chart components as the image below.

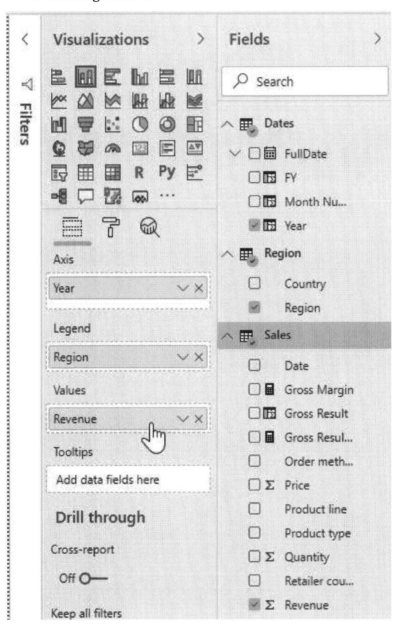

18. Go to **Format** tab, **Legend,** and change **Title** to **Off**.

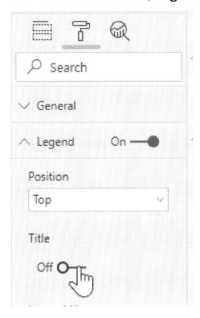

19. Go to **X-Axis** and set the **Text size** to 14.

20. Change **Border** to **On** and select light-gray color.

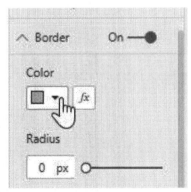

21. Copy and paste the column chart to have three identical.

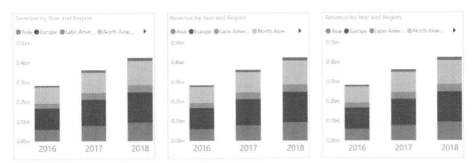

22. Select the column chart in the middle and change to **Clustered column chart**.

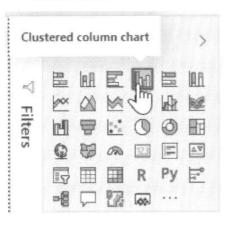

23. Select the third column chart and change to **100% Stacked column chart**.

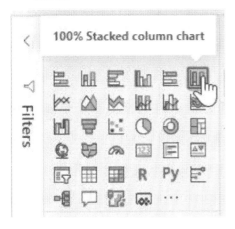

24. The three-column charts should look like the image below.

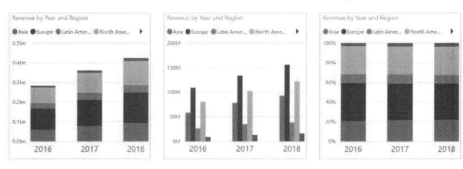

25. Hold **ctrl** key, and click on both **100% Stacked** charts.

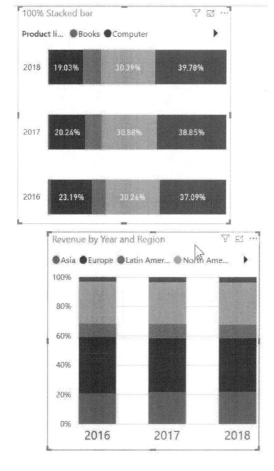

26. Go to **Format** tab, **Align** and click on **Align right**.

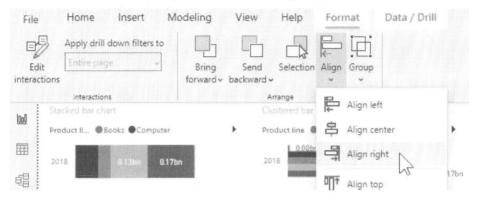

27. Hold **ctrl** key and click on the two charts on the left.

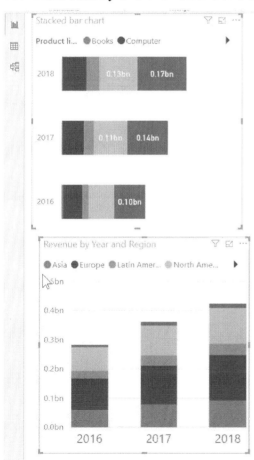

28. Go to **Format** tab, **Align** and click on **Align left**.

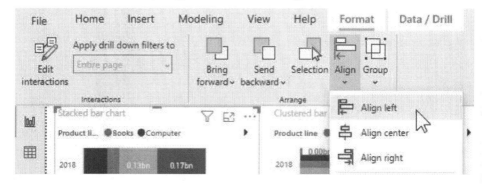

29. Hold **ctrl** key and click on the three top charts.

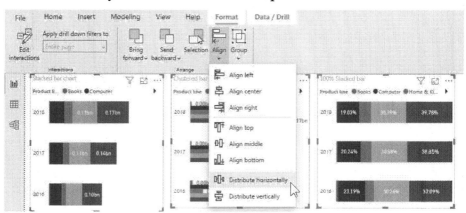

30. Go to **Format** tab, **Align** (Distribute) and click on **Distribute horizontally**.

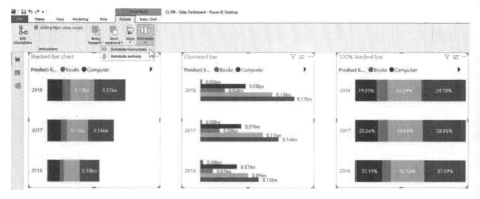

31. Hold **ctrl** key and select the three bottom charts. Go to **Align** and click on bottom. Also, click on **Distribute horizontally.**

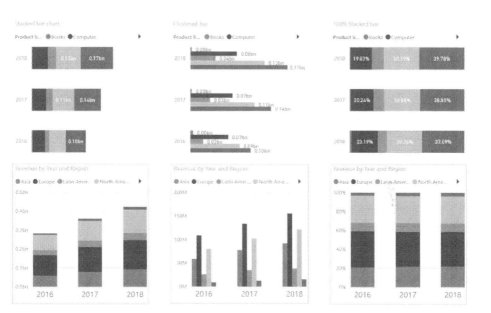

32. If you click on any data, you will see that Power BI will filter the entire dashboard based on your selection. Click again to clear the filter. Try yourself.

33. You can maximize any chart by clicking on **Focus mode.**

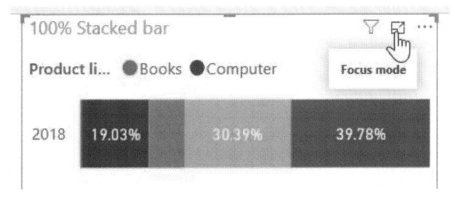

34. Click on **Back to Report** to return.

5.3. Line and Area Chart

1. Click on **Line and Area** tab.

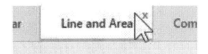

2. Go to Visualizations and go to Line chart.

3. Drag the fields **FullDate**, **Product line,** and **Revenue** to the chart components as the image below.

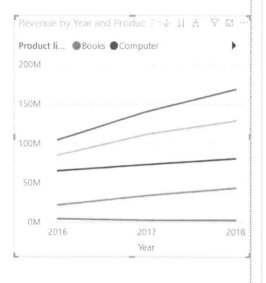
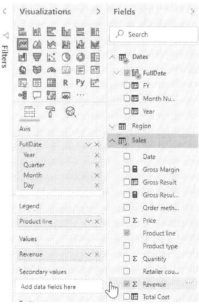

4. Go to **FullDate** component and click on the dropdown button. Select **FullDate**, then, **New group**.

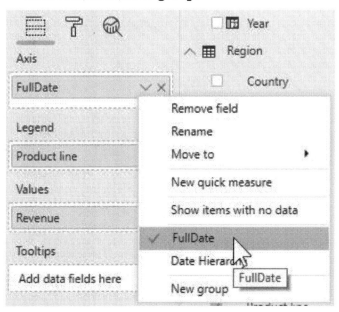

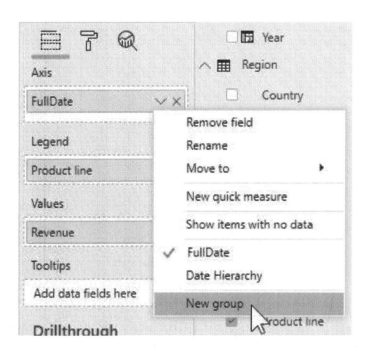

5. In the **Group** window, change the **Bin size** to 1 Month, and click OK.

Groups

Name	FullDate (bins)		Field	FullDate
Group type	Bin	▼	Min value	Friday, 1 January 2016
Bin Type	Size of bins	▼	Max value	Tuesday, 31 December 2019

Binning splits numeric or date/time data into equally sized groups. The default bin size is calculated based on your data.

Bin size | 1   ⇕ | Months   ▼

Reset to default

6. The X-Axis will show months and years (make the chart larger to see it).

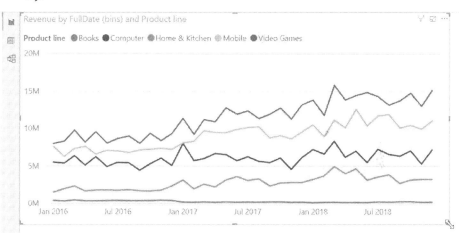

7. Select the chart and click on **Format**. Go to **X-Axis** and change Type to **Categorical**.

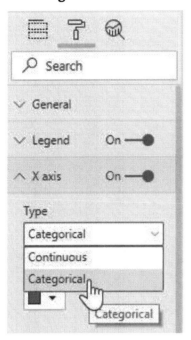

8. The line chart will show every month and year in the range, and a scrollbar.

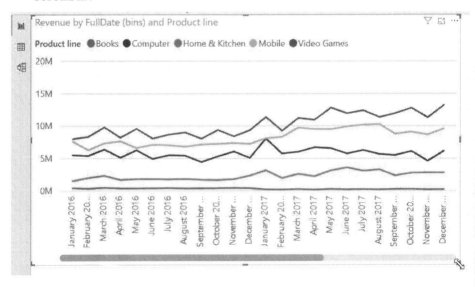

9. Copy the line chart and paste, to have three charts. Drag them to look like the picture below.

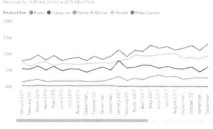

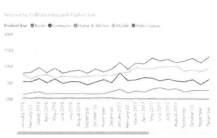
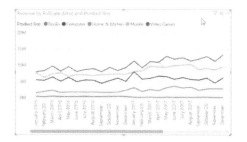

10. Select the second chart and click on **Area Chart**.

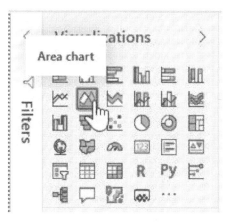

11. Select the third chart and click on **Stacked area chart**.

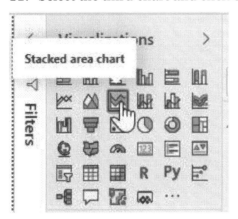

Select the **first** chart and go to **Visualizations, Format**. Go to **Shapes**, change the **Stroke width** to 3, then, change **Line style**, to **Dashed**.

12. Select the **Second** chart and go to **Visualizations, Format.** Go to **Shapes**, change **Stepped**, to **On.**

13. The chart should look like the picture below.

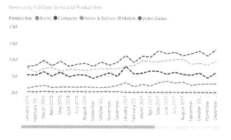

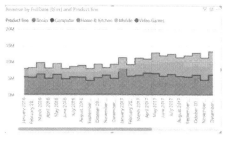

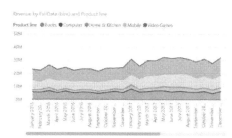

14. Click on a blank area on the canvas, to deselect the chart, and go to **Visualizations** and click on **Slicer**.

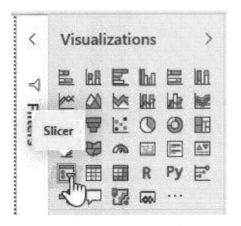

15. Go to **Fields** pane and click on **Date**.

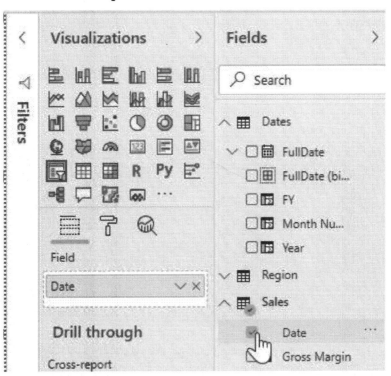

16. Power BI will create a **filter** in a **Slider** format. You can test and see how your data will be filtered as you change the dates. You can drag the slider or pick a date by click on the date fields.

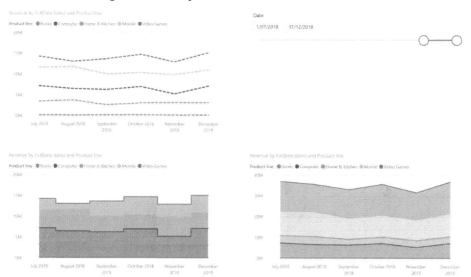

17. Power BI offers several themes that you can choose. Go to **View** tab, **Themes** and test the themes available. Then, select the **Classic Theme**.

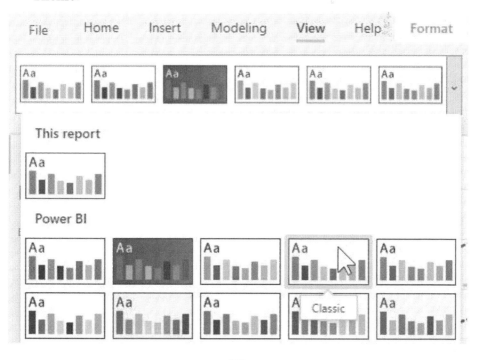

5.4. Combo Charts

1. Select **Combo** tab.

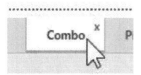

2. Go to Visualizations and click on **Line and stacked column chart**.

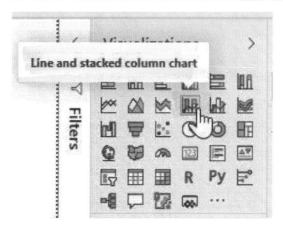

3. Drag the fields **Product line**, **Region** and **Revenue**, and **Quantity** to the chart components as the image below.

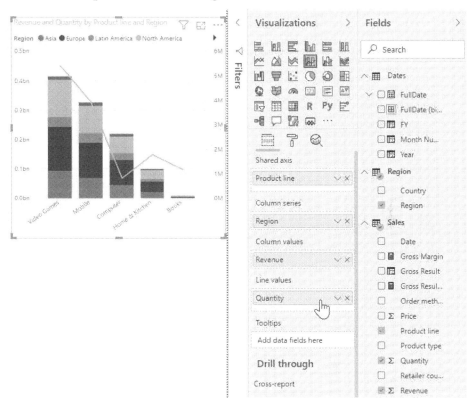

4. Copy the chart and paste, to have three charts.

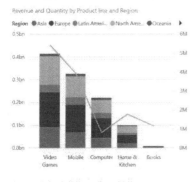

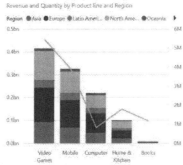
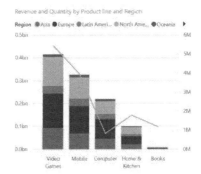

5. Select the second chart, go to **Visualizations** and click on **Line and clustered column chart**.

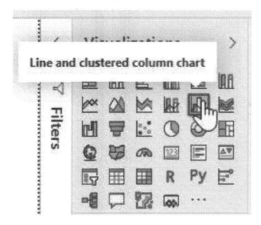

6. Select the third chart, go to **Visualizations** and click on **Ribbon chart**.

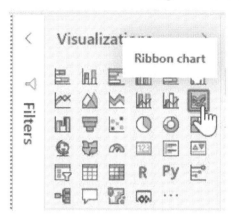

7. The three charts should look like the image below.

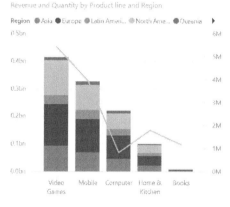

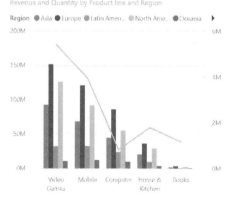

8. Click on a blank area on the canvas, to deselect the chart. Now you can edit the canvas. Go to **Visualizations, Format**.

9. Go to Page Background, change the color to White 20% darker; and Transparency 0%.

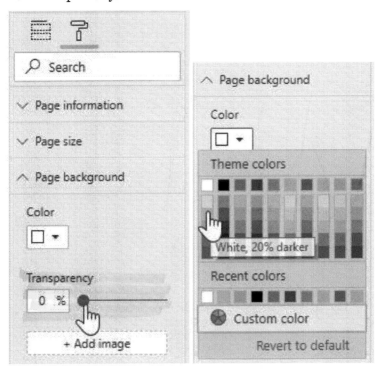

10. Select the first chart, go to **Visualizations**, **Format**, **Background**, change to **ON**, and set the color **White** with **Transparency 0%**.

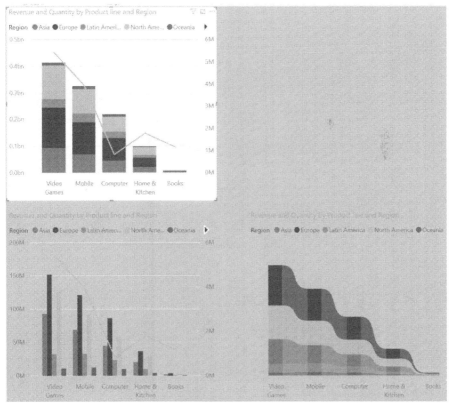

11. Select the second chart and change the **Background** color to blue,
Transparency 50%.

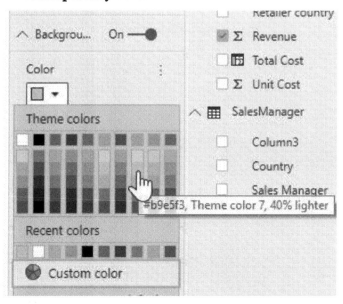

12. Select the third chart and change the **Background** color to purple,
Transparency 70%.

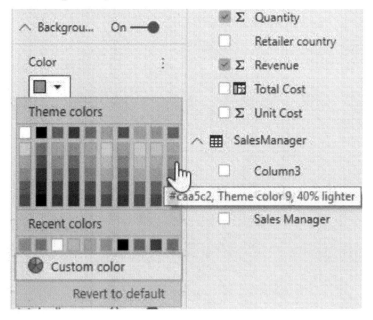

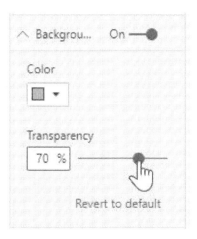

13. The three different backgrounds should look like the image below.

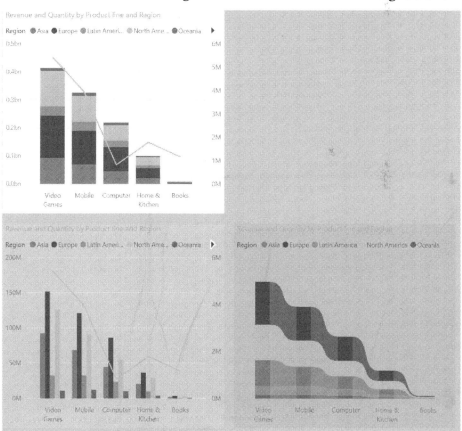

14. Click on a blank area on the canvas, to deselect the chart. Go to **Visualizations** and click on **Slicer** and drag the field **Region** to the **Field** component.

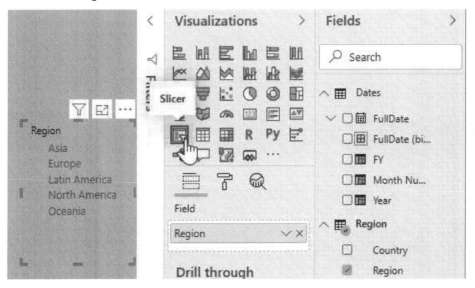

15. Select the slicer, go to **Format, Background** and change the color to white and **Transparency** to 0%.

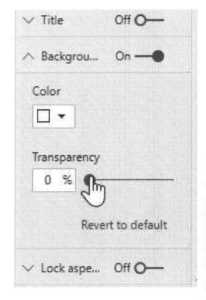

16. Be sure to have the filter as **List** format.

17. Select the slicer, go to **Visualizations**, **Format**, **Selection Controls** and change **Select All** to **On**, **Single Select** to **Off**, and **Multi-select with CTRL** to **OFF**. It will show a "Select All" option in the list and will allow multiple selections.

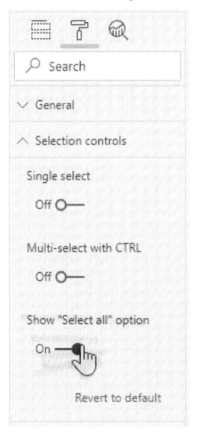

18. Go to **Item** and change **Outline** to **Bottom only**, and **Text size** to 14.

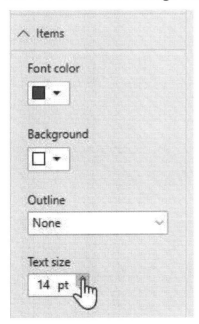

19. Move and resize the objects to look like the image below. Then, test the filter selecting individual values or select all.

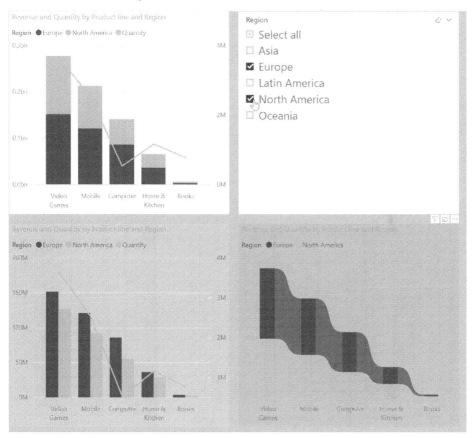

5.5. Treemap, Gauge, Pie and Donut charts

1. Select the **Pie** tab.

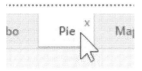

2. Go to Visualizations and click on **Pie chart**. Drag the fields **Product line**, and **Revenue** the chart components as the image below.

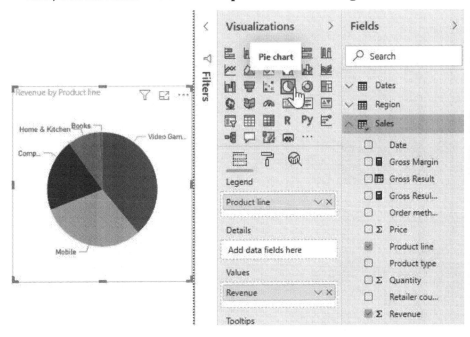

3. Go to **Visualizations**, **Format**, **Data colors,** and change the colors. **Video Games** = Purple, **Mobile** = Green, **Computer** = Yellow, **Home & Kitchen** = Orange, and **Book** = Black.

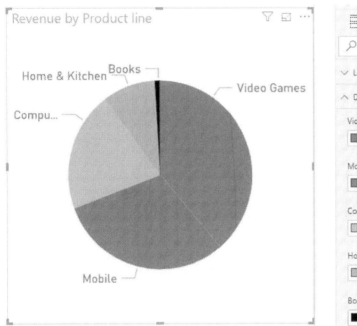

Format

Paintbrush

4. Go to **Detail labels,** and select **All detail labels.**

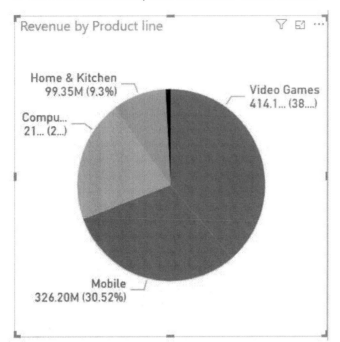
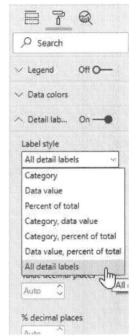

5. Go to **General** and change the **X and Y Position** to 0, and **Width and Height** to 350.

6. Copy the chart and paste to have four charts.

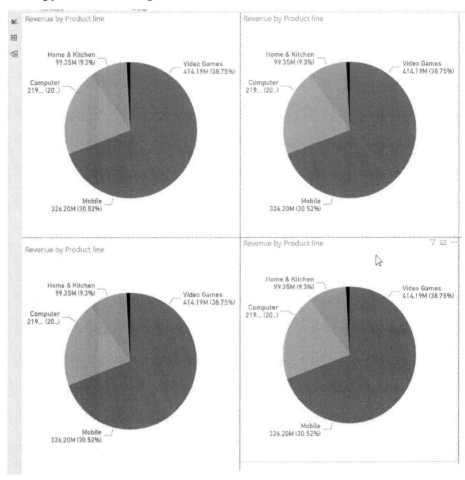

7. Select the chart below the first and click on **Donut chart**

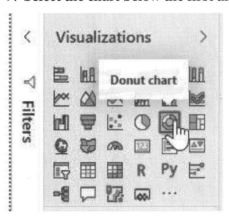

8. Select top right chart and click on **Treemap.**

9. Select the fourth chart and click on **Gauge.**

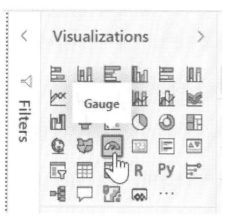

10. The charts should look like the image below.

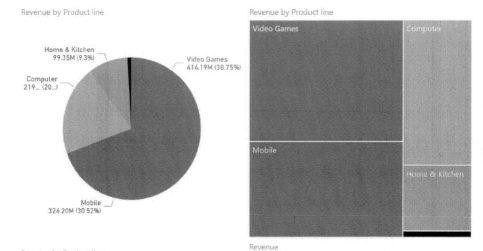

11. Click on a blank area on the canvas, to deselect the chart, and click
    on **Slicer**. Drag the field **Year** to the **Field** component.

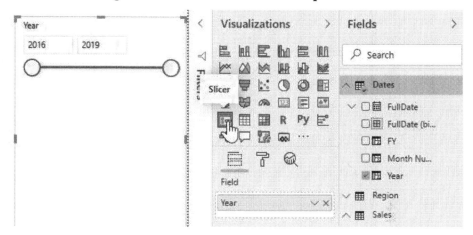

12. Change the type to **Dropdown**.

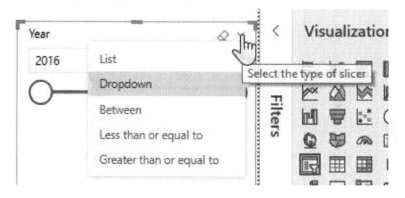

13. Go to **Format, Selection Controls** and change **Single Select** to **On**.

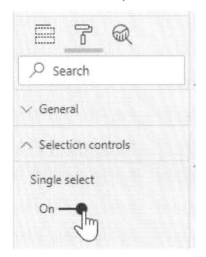

14. Select the Gauge chart, go to **Format, Gauge axis** and set the **Max** as 500000000 (500 Million), and the **Target** as 400000000 (400 Million).

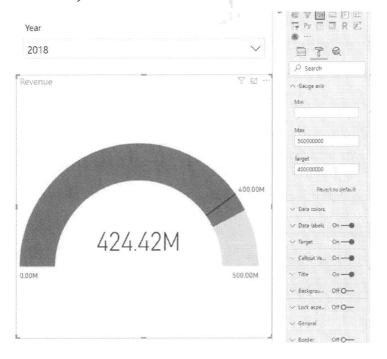

15. Go to **Callout Value** and change **Value decimal places** to 0 (type 0). Also, change Data labels to On.

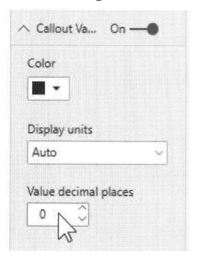

16. Test how to the new slicer works and try to click on the chart area to filter the report.

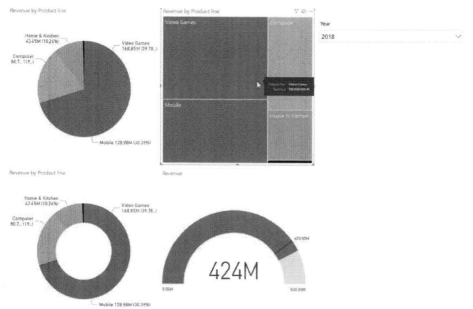

5.6. Maps

1. Select **Maps** tab.

2. Go to **Visualizations** and click on **Map**.

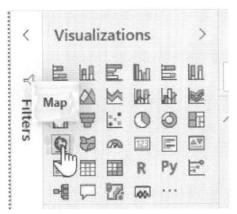

3. Drag the fields **Country**, and **Revenue** to the chart components as the image below.

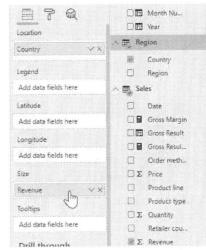

4. Go to Visualizations, Format, Map styles and change the Theme to Light.

5. Go to **General** and change the **X and Y Position** to 0, **Width** to 520, and **Height** to 370.

6. Copy the chart and paste, to have one more chart.

7. Select the new chart, go **Visualizations** and click on **Filled map**. Then, add **Revenue** to the chart component.

8. Click on a blank area on the canvas to deselect the chart. Go **Visualizations** and click on **Slicer**. Drag the **Product line** to field component.

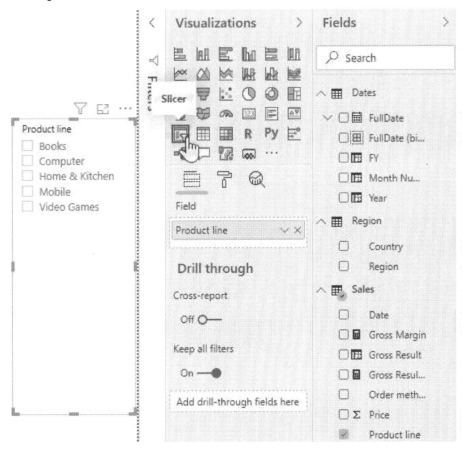

9. Click on a blank area on the canvas to deselect the slicer. Go **Visualizations** and click on **Slicer** again. Drag the **Product type** to field component.

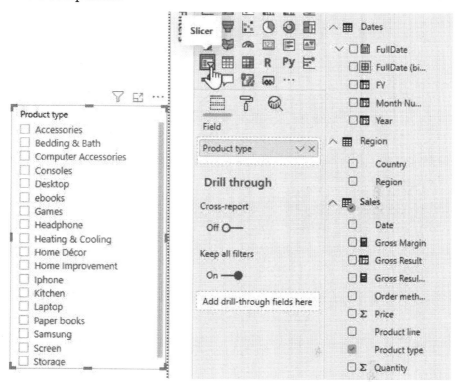

10. Hold **ctrl** and select both slicers. Go to **Format**, **Align,** and click on **Align center**.

11. Click on **Computer** item in the slicer. You will see that it filters the maps and **Product type** filter as well.

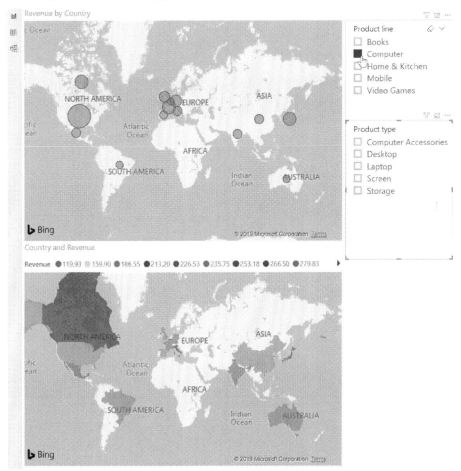

5.7. Cards and tables

1. Select Cards and Tables tab.

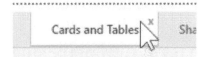

2. Go to **Visualizations** and click on **Card**. Drag the field **Revenue** to the
   chart components as the image below.

3. Go to **Format** tab, **Title** and set it as **On**. Type the title **Global**. Then, change the **Background color** to green, **Font color** to white, **Text size** to 15, and **Center** alignment. Also, change the **Border** to **On**.

4. Click on a blank area on the canvas to deselect the chart.

5. Go to Visualizations and click on **Multi-row card**.

6. Drag the fields **Sales Manager**, **Revenue**, and **Quantity** to the chart components as the image below.

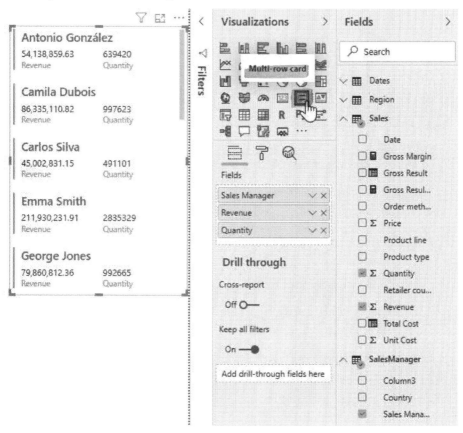

7. Go to **Visualizations**, **Format** tab, **Category labels** and change the Text size to **8**.

8. Go to **Card** and change **Padding** to 2.

9. Click on a blank area on the canvas, to deselect the card.

10. Go to **Visualizations** and click on **Table**.

11. Drag the fields **Sales Manager, Product line, Region, Country,** and **Revenue** to the chart components as the image below.

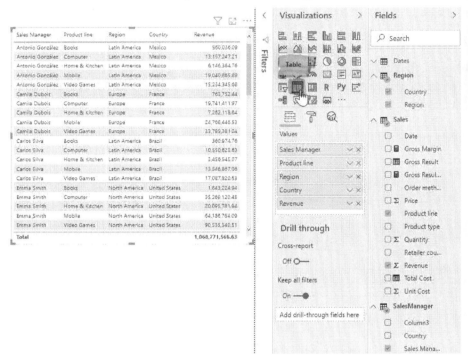

12. Go to **Visualizations**, **Format** tab, **Style,** and change the style to **Condensed**.

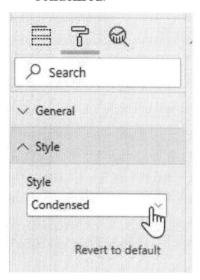

13. Go to Conditional formatting, select **Revenue**, and set **Data bars** to On.

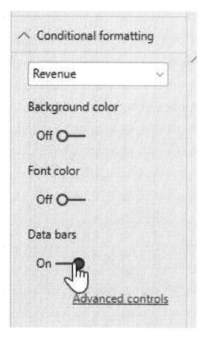

14. The table should be looking as the image below.

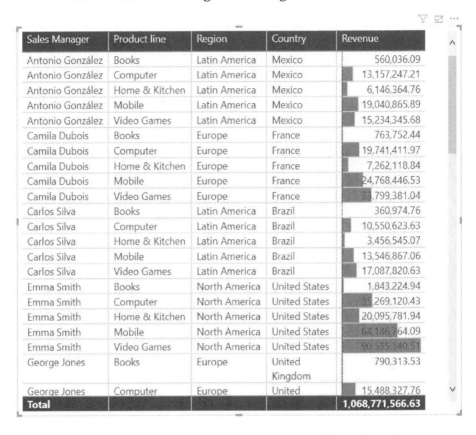

Sales Manager	Product line	Region	Country	Revenue
Antonio González	Books	Latin America	Mexico	560,036.09
Antonio González	Computer	Latin America	Mexico	13,157,247.21
Antonio González	Home & Kitchen	Latin America	Mexico	6,146,364.76
Antonio González	Mobile	Latin America	Mexico	19,040,865.89
Antonio González	Video Games	Latin America	Mexico	15,234,345.68
Camila Dubois	Books	Europe	France	763,752.44
Camila Dubois	Computer	Europe	France	19,741,411.97
Camila Dubois	Home & Kitchen	Europe	France	7,262,118.84
Camila Dubois	Mobile	Europe	France	24,768,446.53
Camila Dubois	Video Games	Europe	France	33,799,381.04
Carlos Silva	Books	Latin America	Brazil	360,974.76
Carlos Silva	Computer	Latin America	Brazil	10,550,623.63
Carlos Silva	Home & Kitchen	Latin America	Brazil	3,456,545.07
Carlos Silva	Mobile	Latin America	Brazil	13,546,867.06
Carlos Silva	Video Games	Latin America	Brazil	17,087,820.63
Emma Smith	Books	North America	United States	1,843,224.94
Emma Smith	Computer	North America	United States	35,269,120.43
Emma Smith	Home & Kitchen	North America	United States	20,095,781.94
Emma Smith	Mobile	North America	United States	64,186,764.09
Emma Smith	Video Games	North America	United States	90,535,340.51
George Jones	Books	Europe	United Kingdom	790,313.53
George Jones	Computer	Europe	United	15,488,327.76
Total				1,068,771,566.63

15. Copy the table and paste, to have one more table. Select the new table, go to **Visualizations** and click on **Matrix**.

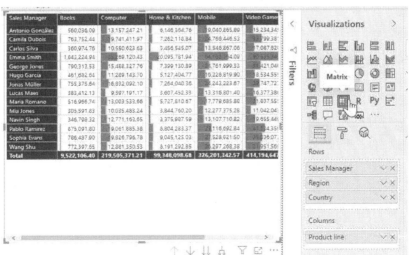

16. Change the column size as you wish.

17. Click on a blank area on the canvas to deselect the slicer. Go
Visualizations and click on **Slicer** again. Drag the **FY** to field
component.

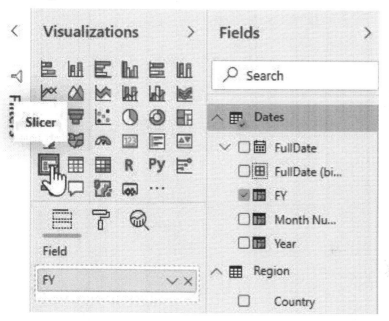

18. Change the slicer style to **Dropdown**.

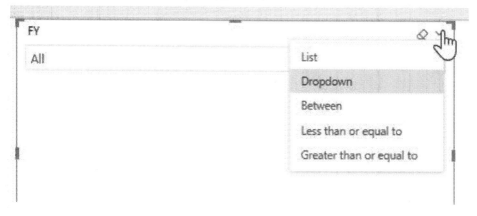

19. Your Cards and Tables should look like the image below.

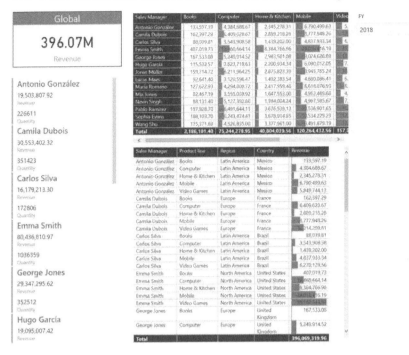

5.8. Shapes and Images

1. Select **Shapes and Images** tab.

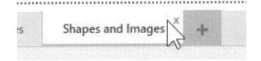

2. Go **Insert tab, Shapes** and select **Rectangle**.

3. Power BI will automatically create the shape.

4. Select the new rectangle and go to **Format Shape, Line** and change **Weight** to 0 pt, and **Round edges** to 15 px.

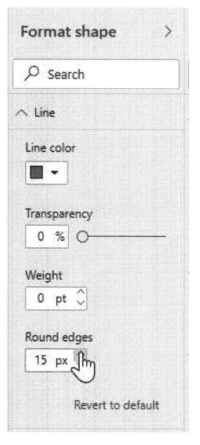

5. Go to Fill and change Fill color to **Black, 20% lighter**.

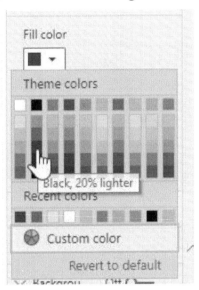

6. Go to **General** and change the **X and Y Position** to 0, **Width** to 600, and **Height** to 100.

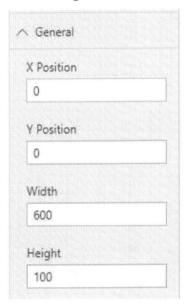

7. Click on a blank area on the canvas to deselect the shape.

8. Go to **Insert** tab, and select **Text box**.

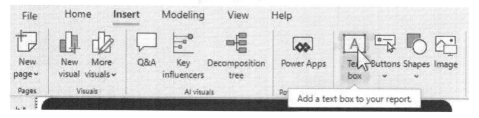

9. Type **Create and Learn**. Select the text and change the **color** to amber, **Bold, Center,** and **size** to 20.

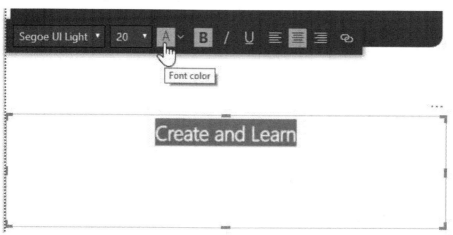

10. Go to Visualizations, Background and change to Off.

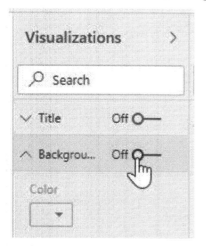

11. Move the text over the shape and use the red guidelines to align it horizontally and vertically.

12. Visit the address createandlearn.net/bifiles and download the logo.png

13. Go to **Insert tab**, and click on **Image**.

14. Select the downloaded image: logo.png

15. Go to **Insert** tab, **Buttons**. Then, select **Left arrow**.

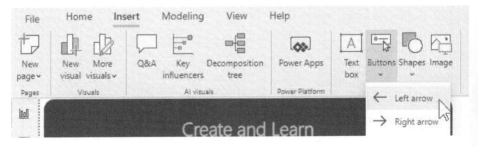

16. Select the arrow image and go to **Visualizations**, **Actions** and change to **On** and type **Back.**

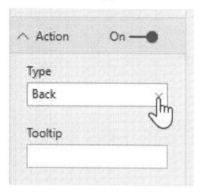

17. Hold **ctrl** and **click** on the arrow to go to the previous tab. You can try different actions.

5.9. Custom Visuals

Power BI allows you to add new visuals from custom files or from the marketplace.

Most Custom visuals are created by third-part companies, so Microsoft notifies that they cannot guarantee. Talk to your IT department to decide whether or not you should be using those in your company.

The custom visuals are located under the item **Get more visuals**.

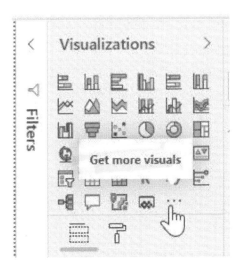

And it is possible to import from a file or Import from marketplace.

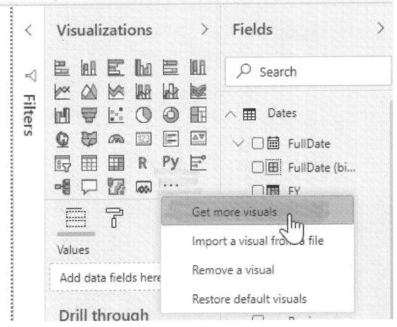

The Market place has a list of free visuals, and it is continuously updated.

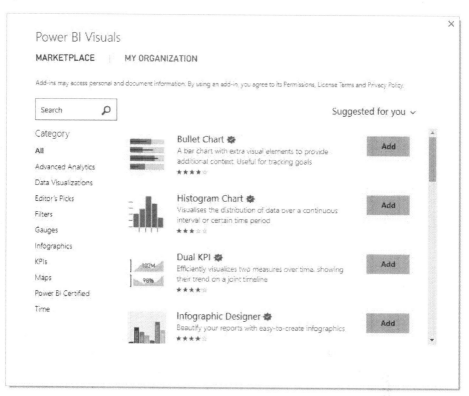

In this example, I have included the Radar Chart by clicking on **Add**.

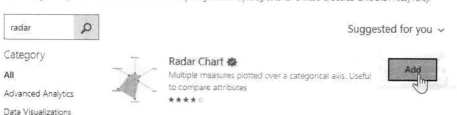

Now I have a new item on my **Visualizations** pane called **Radar Chart 1.3.1**.

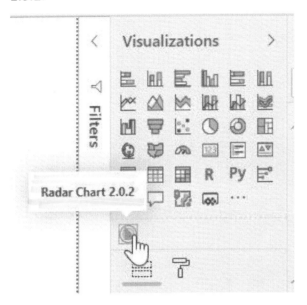

In this chart, I have included the **Product line** and **Revenue**.

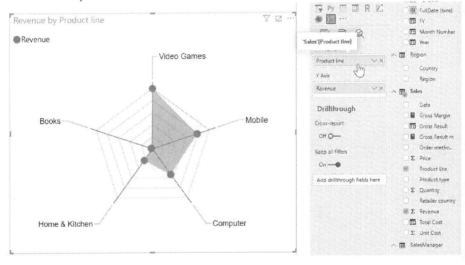

If you want to delete the custom visual, just click on **Get more visuals** and select **Remove a visual**.

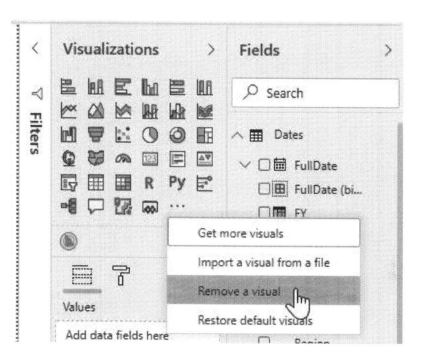

6. Sales Dashboard

Before starting this chapter, you need to conclude chapter 3 Get Data, and Chapter 4 Model data. These chapters will give you all the **data, custom columns**, and **measures** required to proceed.

1. Select the **Dashboard** tab.

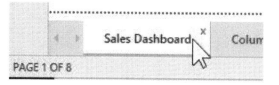

2. Click on a blank area on the canvas. Go to **Visualizations, Format**.

3. Go to **Page Background** and choose light-gray color (White 20% Darker), and **Transparency** of 60%. Also, set the **Page size, Type** to 16:9.

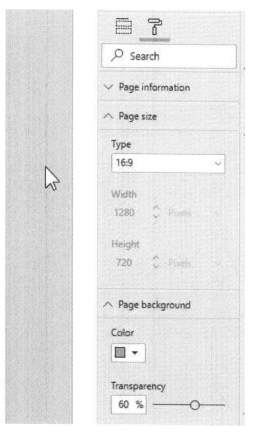

4. Go **Insert** tab, and click on **Image**.

5. Select the logo.png

6. Go to **Format image** pane, **Background,** and change to **On**. Select white color and transparency 0%.

7. Go to **General** and change the **X Position** to 5, **Y Position** to 6, **Width** to 274, and **Height** to 142.

8. Click on a blank area on the canvas to deselect the image. Go to **Visualizations** and click on **Card**.

9. Drag the field **Revenue** to the card component.

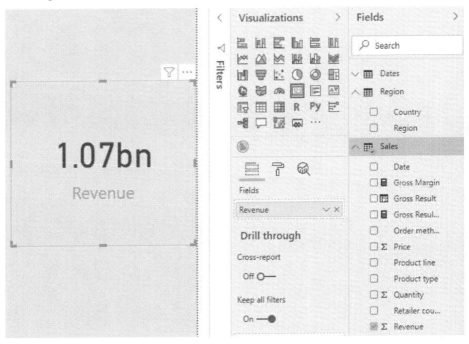

10. Go to **Visualizations**, **Format**, Background, and change to **On**. Select white color and transparency 0%.

11. Go to **General** and change the **X Position** to 284, **Y Position** to 6, Width to 182, and **Height** to 142.

12. Copy the card and paste, to have three cards.

13. Select the second card and change the field **component** to **Total Cost**.

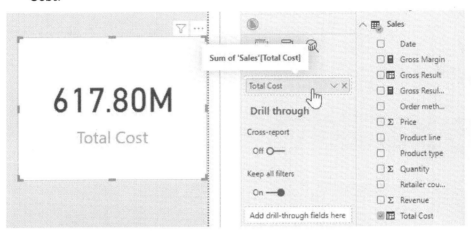

14. Go to **Format** tab, **General** and change the **X Position** to 470, **Y Position** to 6, **Width** to 182 and **Height** to 142.

15. Select the third card and change the field **component** to **Gross Margin**.

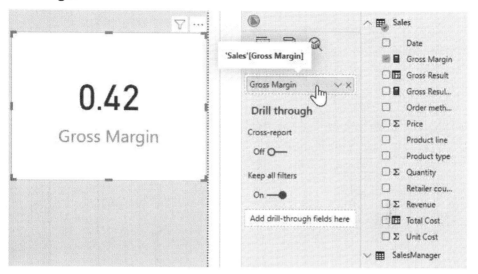

16. Go to **Fields** pane and click on **Gross Margin**.

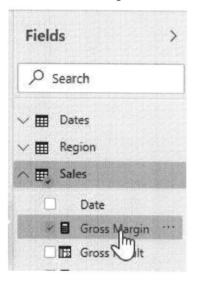

17. Go to **Measure tools** tab and select **Percentage format**, and change decimal places to 0.

18. Go to **General** and change the **X Position** to 657, **Y Position** to 6, **Width** to 182, and **Height** to 142.

19. Your dashboard should look like the image below.

Create and Learn	1.07bn	617.80M	42%
createandlearn.net	Revenue	Total Cost	Gross Margin

20. Go to **Insert** tab, **Shapes** and click on **Rectangle**.

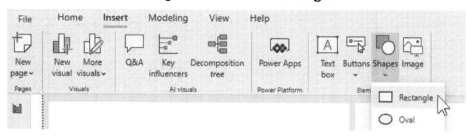

21. Select the new rectangle and go to **Format Shape, Line** and change **Weight** to 0 pt, and **Round edges** to 0 px.

22. Go to **Fill** and change to Off. Go to **Background** and change to **On**. Select white **color** and **transparency** 0%.

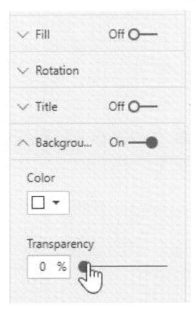

23. Go to **General** and change the **X Position** to 845, **Y Position** to 6, **Width** to 428, and **Height** to 142.

24. Click on a blank area on the canvas to deselect the chart.

25. Go to **Visualizations** and click on **Slicer**. Drag the fields **Date** to the slicer components as the image below.

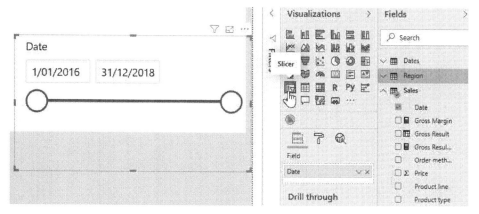

26. Go to **General** and change the **X Position** to 863, **Y Position** to 9, **Width** to 258, and **Height** to 76. Then, go to **Background** and change to **On**. Select white **color** and **transparency** 0%.

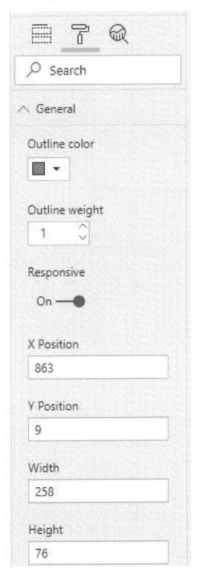

27. Click on a blank area on the canvas to deselect the chart.

28. Go to **Visualizations** and click on **Slicer**. Drag the fields **Product line** to the slicer components as the image below.

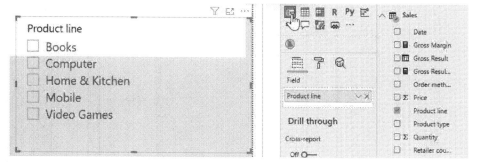

29. Go to **General** and change the **Y Position** to 79, **Width** to 259, **Height** to 58 and **X Position** to 865.

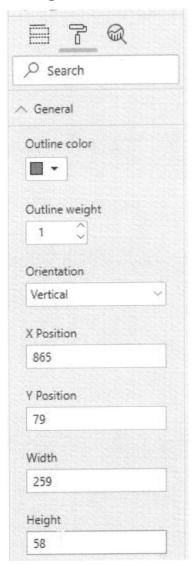

30. Change the slice style to **Dropdown**.

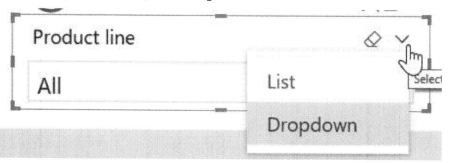

31. Click on a blank area on the canvas to deselect the slicer.

Go to **Visualizations** and click on **Slicer**. Drag the field **Region** to the slicer components as the image below.

32. Go to **General** and change the **Y Position** to 6, **Width** to 145, **Height** to 143, and **X Position** to 1128.

33. Go to Selection Controls and change Show Select All option to On; and Single Select to Off.

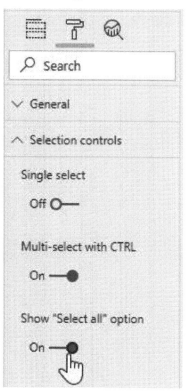

34. Your dashboard should look like the image below.

35. Click on a blank area on the canvas to deselect the chart.

36. Go to **Visualizations** and click on **Clustered column chart**. Drag the fields **Year**, and **Revenue** to the slicer components as the image below.

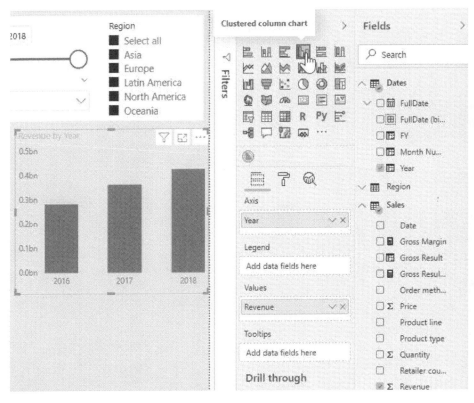

37. Go to **Visualizations, Format** tab, **General,** and change the **X Position** to 5, **Y Position** to 153, **Width** to 274, and **Height** to 270. Also, turn the **Y axis** off.

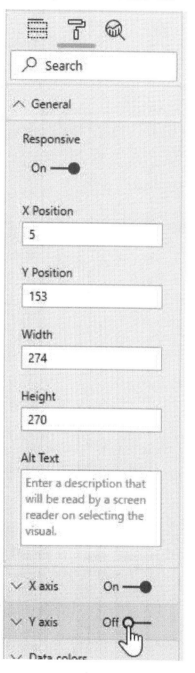

38. Go to **Data labels** change to On, **Display units** to Millions, and **Value decimal places** to 0 (type 0).

39. Go to **Data colors** and select the color as the image below (Dark Gray).

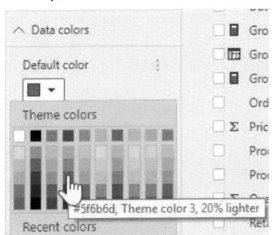

40. Go to **Background** and change to **On**. Select white **color** and **transparency** 0%.

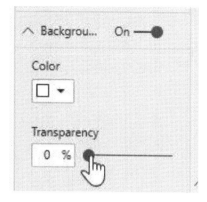

41. Click on a blank area on the canvas, to deselect the chart.

Go to **Visualizations** and click on **Line Chart**. Drag the fields **FullDate (bins)**, **Region**, **Revenue** to the slicer components as the image below.

If you missed the **FullDate (bins)** creation, check steps in the **Line and Area Chart** chapter.

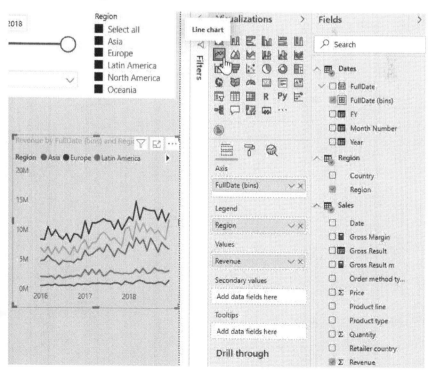

42. Go to **Visualizations**, **Format** tab, **X-Axis**, and change Type to Categorical.

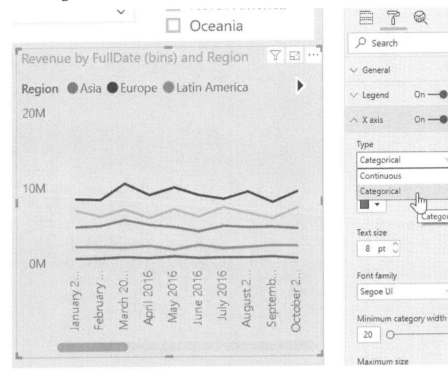

43. Go to **General** and change the **X Position** to 284, **Y Position** to 153, Width to 555, and **Height** to 270.

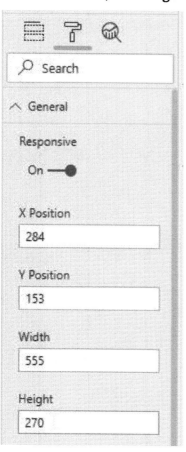

44. Go to **Background** and change to **On.** Select white **color** and **transparency** 0%.

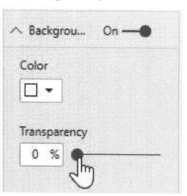

45. Change the data range to 01-January-2018 to 31-December-2018.

46. You will note that the **Revenue by Year** is filtered and showing only 2018.

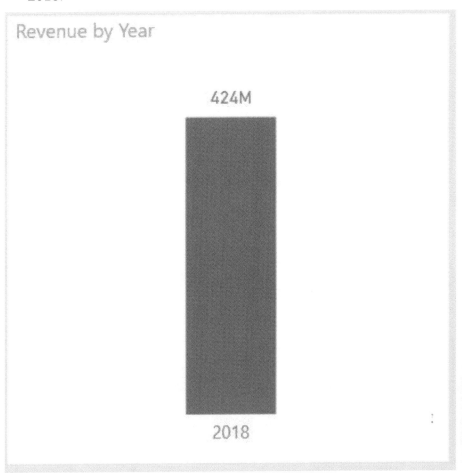

47. Select the chart **Revenue by Year**. Then, go to **Format** tab and click on **Edit Interactions**.

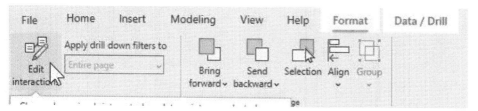

48. Select the date slicer to change any interaction affected by this slicer.

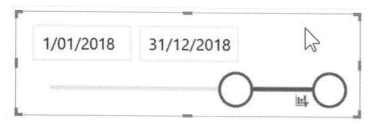

49. On the bar chart, check the interactions as **None**. It means that this chart will not be affected when you change the date slicer.

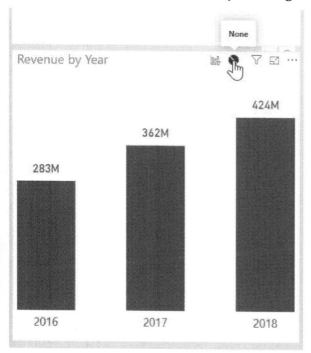

50. Go to **Format** tab and deselect **Edit interactions.**

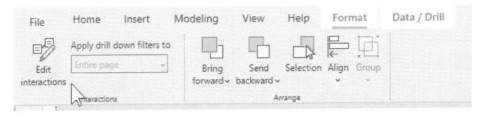

51. Your dashboard should look like the image below.

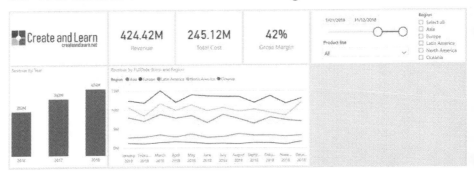

52. Click on a blank area on the canvas to deselect the chart.

53. Go to **Visualizations** and click on **Map.** Drag the fields **Retailer country, Region,** and **Revenue** to the slicer components as the image below.

54. Go to **Visualizations, Format** tab, **General,** and change the **X Position** to 845, **Y Position** to 153, **Width** to 428, and **Height** to 270.

55. Go to **Map styles, Theme,** and select **Light**. Then, go to **Background** and change to **On**. Select white **color** and **transparency** 0%.

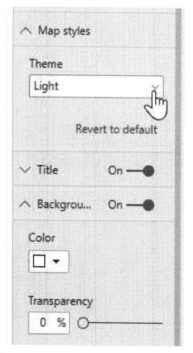

56. Click on a blank area on the canvas to deselect the map.

57. Go to **Visualizations** and click on **Donut chart**. Drag the fields **Order method type** and **Revenue** to the slicer components as the image below.

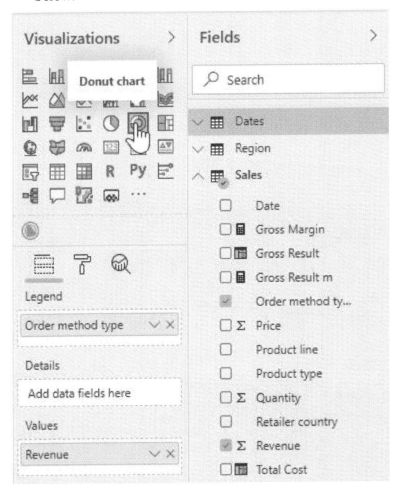

58. Go to **Format**, **Detail labels**, Label style, and select **Category, data value**.

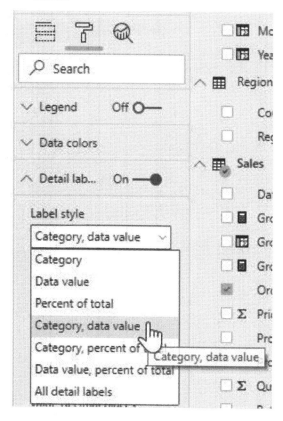

59. Go to **Background** and change to **On**. Select white **color** and **transparency** 0%.

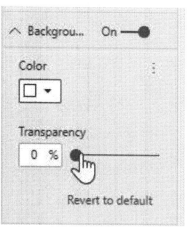

60. Go to **General** and change the **X Position** to 5, **Y Position** to 428, **Width** to 274, and **Height** to 286.

61. Go to **Data colors** and select the colors as below (**Web** Green, **Sales Visit** Dark Grey, **E-mail** Ochre, **Telephone** Gray, **Fax** Red, and **Mail** blue).

62. Click on a blank area on the canvas to deselect the chart.

63. Go to **Visualizations** and click on **Card**. Drag the field **Revenue** to the slicer components as the image below.

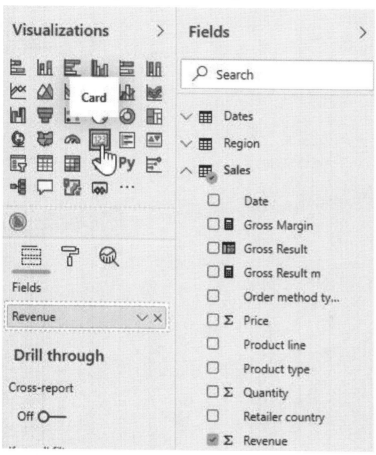

64. Go to **Visualizations, Format** tab, **General** and change the **X Position** to 52, **Width** to 180 and **Height** to 142 and **Y Position** to 503.

65. Go to **Data label** and change decimal places to 0. *Tip: Sometimes, you need to increase to 1 and return to 0.

66. Go to **Category label** and change to **Off**.

67. Your dashboard should look like the image below.

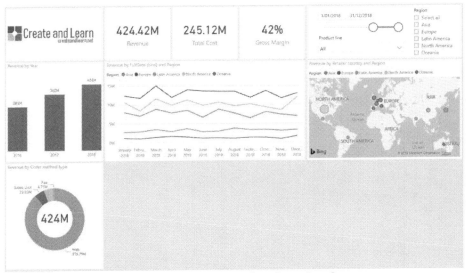

Click on a blank area on the canvas, to deselect the chart.

68. Go to **Visualizations** and click on **Treemap**. Drag the fields **Product line, Product type**, and **Revenue** to the slicer components as the image below.

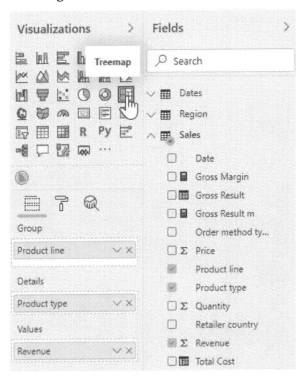

69. Go to **Visualizations, Format** tab, **Background,** and change to **On.** Select white **color** and **transparency** 0%.

70. Go to **General** and change the **X Position** to 284, **Y Position** to 428, **Width** to 555, and **Height** to 286.

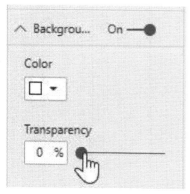

71. Click on a blank area on the canvas to deselect the chart.

72. Go to **Visualizations** and click on **Stacked bar chart**. Drag the fields **Sales Manager, Country, Product line, Region,** and **Revenue** to the slicer components as the image below.

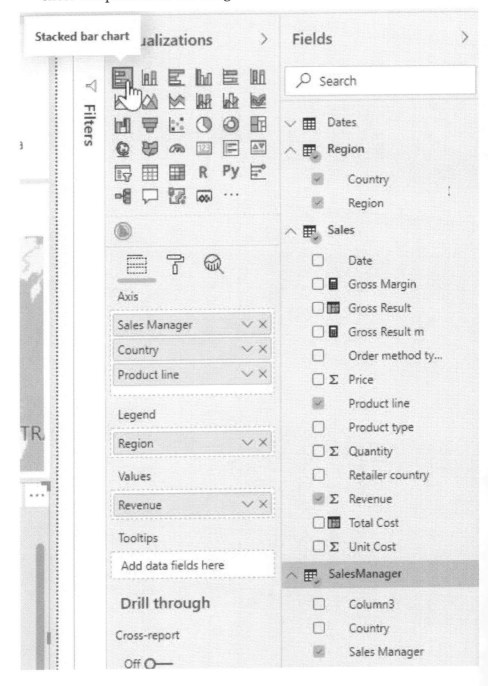

73. Go to **Visualizations**, **Format** tab, **General,** and change the **X Position** to 844, **Y Position** to 427, **Width** to 430 and **Height** to 288. Change **Data labels** to **On**.

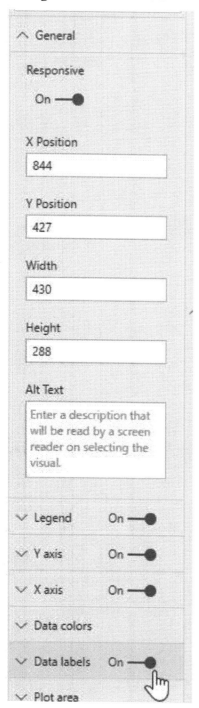

74. Go to **Background** and change to **On**. Select white **color** and **transparency** 0%.

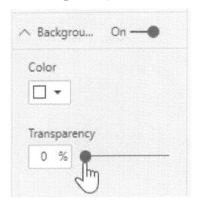

75. The dashboard should look like the image below.

76. To create a mobile dashboard, go to **View** tab, and click on **Phone Layout** or **Mobile Layout**.

77. Move the **visuals** from **Visualizations** pane into the mobile layout. You can resize and change the order the way you want.

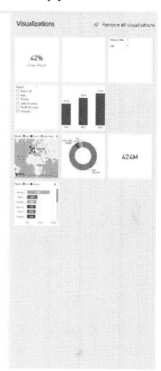

78. To go back, click on **Mobile Layout** (Desktop Layout).

79. Click on the **Filters** arrow to expand the pane.

80. Drag the **Sales Manager** field to the **Add data fields here** section in the **Filters** pane. This action will allow you to create a fast filter to your dashboard.

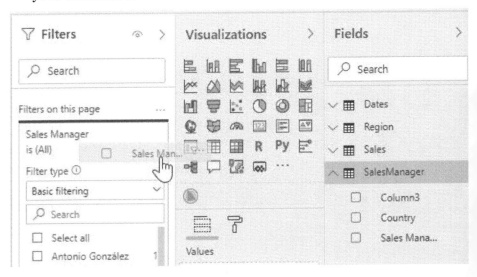

7. Bookmarks

In Power BI you can use bookmarks to capture a specific configured view including visuals and filters.

It is useful to create a **Clean Filter** effect or to create a collection of bookmarks to be presented in a story sequence.

1. Go to **View** tab and select **Bookmarks Pane**.

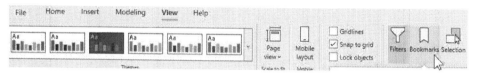

2. Go to the **Bookmarks** pane and click on **Add**.

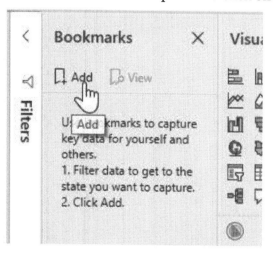

3. Double-click the **Bookmark 1** and type the new name **Standard view**. This will save the current dashboard satuts into this bookmark.

4. Go to **Insert** tab, and click on **Buttons**. Then, select **Reset**.

5. Go to **General** and change the **X position** to 1043, **Y Position** to 15, **Width** to 48 and **Height** to 32.

6. Switch **Action** to **On**. Then, go to **Type** and select **Bookmark**. Then, go to **Bookmark** and select **Standard view**.

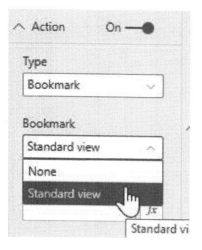

7. Change the filters as the image below.

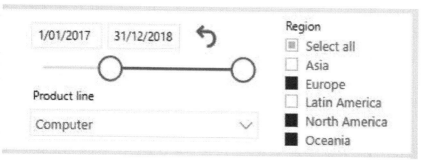

8. To return to the first bookmark created, hold **CTRL** key and **click** on the **reset** button.

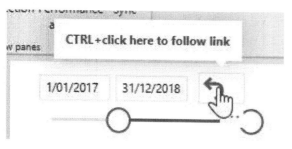

9. Deselect the **Bookmarks** option.

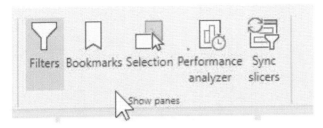

10. **Congratulations**! Your dashboard is finished and ready to be shared or published.

11. Click on **Save**.

8. Share Your Work

8.1. Publishing in Power BI service

1. Go to **Home** tab and click on **Publish**.

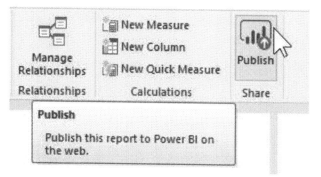

2. You can **Sign in** with your user, or you can create a new one by clicking on **Try for free**.

3. Once logged in, select **My workspace** and click on **Select**.

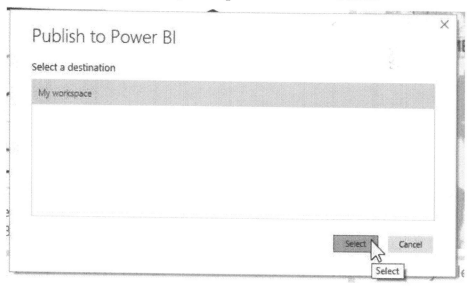

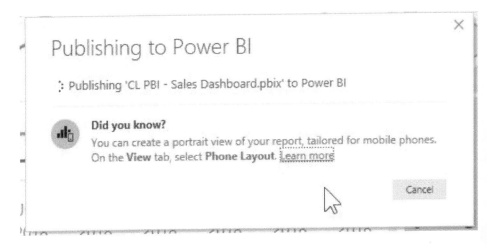

4. Wait till you see the **Success** message. Click on **Open 'CL PBI – Sales Dashboard.pbix' in Power BI**.

5. Although it is the first time, we are publishing this dashboard. It is good to know that every time you republish it, Power BI will ask if you want to replace dataset as the image below.

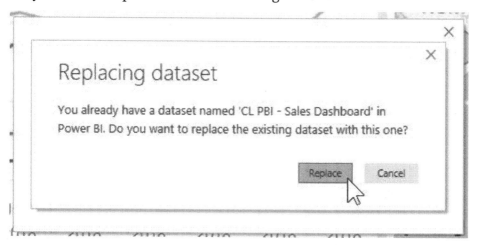

8.2. Share and Publish to Web

1. To access Power BI service go to https://app.powerbi.com

2. Sign In with your account.

3. The dashboard created in Power BI Desktop will sit in the **Reports** area. Click on it.

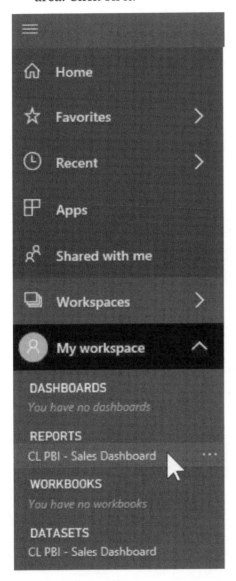

4. Power BI is updating the looking and feel, to see it, set the **New look** to **On**.

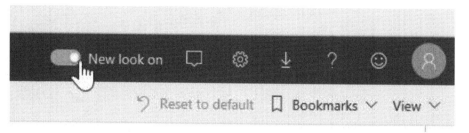

5. Below is the new look with the **CL PBI – Sales Dashboard** selected.

6. Click on the ellipsis icon and select **Edit**

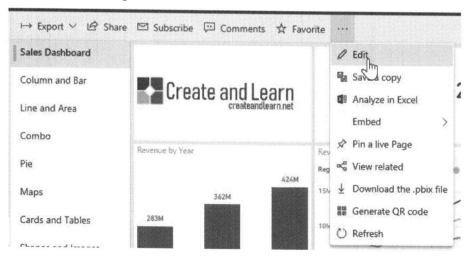

7. Right-click all the tabs, except the Sales Dashboard, and click on **Hide Page**. You will do this, so it will not appear when you share.

8. Click on Sales Dashboard tab.

9. You can click on **Mobile Layout** if you need to edit the mobile dashboard.

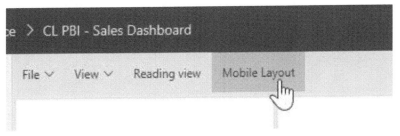

10. Click on **Reading view** to go back.

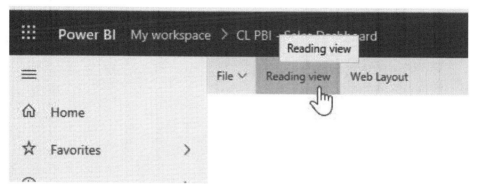

11. If the **Unsaved changes** message appears, click on **Save**.

12. Click on **Share** and select **Report**.

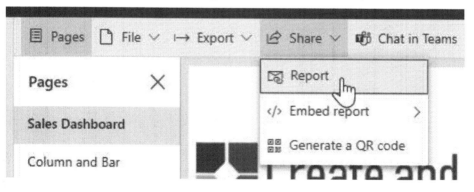

13. Here you have the option to insert the e-mail from a company member and share your dashboard. Note that you can customize a message of invitation, and limit if the user can share your material.

14. Another option to share your dashboard, mentioned in this book, is through **Embed report**. Click on **Share**, **Embed report**, and select **Website or portal**.

15. It will create an embed code that you can include on your website. *Note that this will share with the public, it is **not recommended** to use this function when you have sensitive data, that you do not want to share with the public.

16. You can share through a link or use an HTML code. Also, you can select the size.

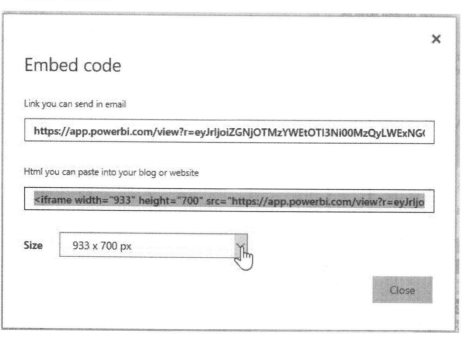

17. In this example, I am using the code on my website.

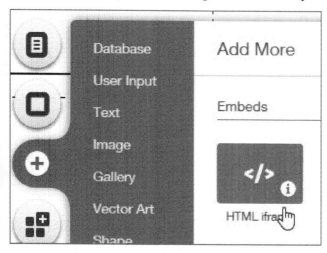

18. Here, I have included the copied HTML generated by Power BI service.

19. Visit https://www.createandlearn.net/pbi to see the result.

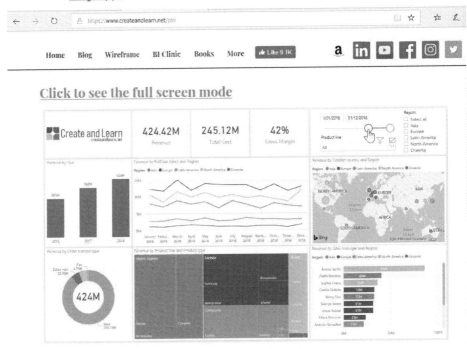

9. Next Steps

1- This book was created to help you to learn by doing and through practice and to expand your knowledge in Power BI.

If you want to keep practicing and improving your knowledge in Power BI through several industries, I have few recommendations:

1- Modify the current dashboard. Try using other types of graphics, fonts, themes, and visuals from the marketplace.

2- Try to build the dashboard for this book without assistance. Get the data, create the relationships, columns and calculated measures, build the dashboard, and publish. Refer to this book only when necessary.

3- Try the **Power BI Academy**, book series, where each book will introduce you to different industry metrics and datasets.

Visit the page createandlearn.net/bi-academy to have access to these books and more.

4- Spread the word. Share your dashboard with colleagues and on social media like LinkedIn. Add me to your network so I can comment and check your progress, on LinkedIn you will find me as Roger F. Silva.

5- Visit the BI Clinic Blog to access extra materials related to this book. https://www.createandlearn.net/biclinicposts

6- Do not stop! Learning has never been more accessible. Search websites, books, videos, and don't stop studying. This is an excellent way to maintain a healthy brain and a promising career!

10. Final words

Thank you for the journey! I hope that you have enjoyed learning from this book as much as I have enjoyed writing and teaching the contents of this book.

Although the Business Intelligence concept is not new, the tools and methods have changed dramatically in recent years, and you made the right decision to gain more knowledge about this software.

What do you think of this book? I would like to ask you to take a minute to **review** my book. Reviews are incredibly important for my work.

If you have any comments or suggestions, please send me an e-mail or a message and **connect with me on LinkedIn** — I would love to hear from you and have you in my network.

Thank you for the time we spent creating and learning.

Roger F. Silva

contact.createandlearn@gmail.com

createandlearn.net

www.linkedin.com/in/roger-f-silva

You can find more Create and Learn books, files, articles, and videos:

https://www.createandlearn.net/

https://www.amazon.com/Roger-F-Silva/e/B07JC8J1L5/

http://www.facebook.com/excelcreateandlearn

https://www.linkedin.com/company/create-and-learn

https://www.instagram.com/createandlearn_net/

https://www.youtube.com/c/createandlearn

For more **Create and Learn** books, visit
https://www.createandlearn.net/:

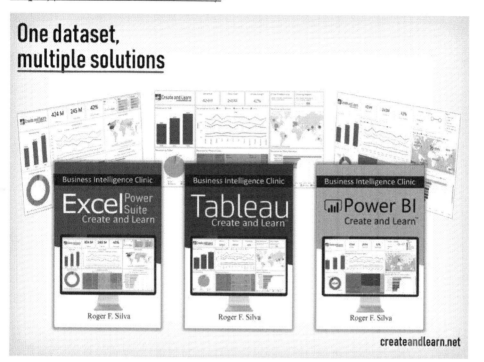

Made in the USA
Middletown, DE
18 December 2020